INSTRUCTOR'S MANUAL AND TEST ITEM FILE

FOURTH EDITION

MAURICE LEGAULT
Southern Illinois University

Music

DANIEL T. POLITOSKE
University of Kansas

ART ESSAYS BY MARTIN WERNER
Temple University

PRENTICE HALL
Englewood Cliffs, New Jersey 07632

© 1988 by **PRENTICE-HALL, INC.**
A Division of Simon & Schuster
Englewood Cliffs, N.J. 07632

ISBN: 0-13-607706-4

Printed in the United States of America

CONTENTS

CHAPTER 1

MELODY AND RHYTHM

Summary

Chapter 1 presents material intended to develop the students' perception of basic musical sounds. Included are found the organizing, disciplining, and refining of the basic material found in melodic shape, phrase structure of melody, rhythmic patterns, meters, and syncopation. For a musical work is essentially a disciplined and refined organization of sounds.

Basic music vocabulary might include: sound, time, noise, musical tone, pitch, staff, upward or downward movement, disjunct or conjunct melody, intervals, contrast, repetition, phrases, melodic and rhythmic patterns, meter, beat, accent, triple and duple meters, measures, subdivision, syncopation, rhythmic motion, tempo, and tempo changes.

Goals and Suggestions for Classroom Experiences

To understand the visual and aural perception of basic melodic and rhythmic musical sounds.

To understand that most music contains these basic melodic and rhythmic sounds.

To understand that melody and rhythm may occur as contrast, repetition, or variation.

1. The whirlwind "Finale" of Chopin's Piano Sonata No. 2 in D♭ Minor, Op. 35 provides a splendid illustration of how tension may be alternately increased and slackened by ascents and descents in a melodic line.

2. Several well-known melodies are used in the textbook to illustrate melodic shapes, the grouping of phrases into melodies, and the repetition of rhythmic patterns to create unity. Additional examples of familiar tunes can be used for the same purpose, preferably notated and distributed to the students, however limited their ability to read music may be at this point.

3. The "Variation de Polymnie" from Stravinsky's ballet Apollon Musagéte can serve to illustrate the unsettling effect of frequent meter changes. This example is particularly useful since the quarter note remains the beat unit throughout, and the shifts are simply alternations of $\frac{2}{4}$

1

and $\frac{3}{4}$. The students will benefit from preparation, for listening to the movement by clapping various patterns of $\frac{2}{4}$ and $\frac{3}{4}$ measures as you conduct them. As the movement is played, continued use of the conducting pattern will help the students observe the shifts more readily.

4. A rhythmically expressive performance requires flexibility, even in fast, uncomplicated music. A metronome set to accompany a movement such as the opening "Allegro" of Schubert's Symphony No. 5 in B^b Major, D. 485 will allow the class to observe how quickly and frequently deviations from the strict mentronomic beat occur.

5. The students should understand that tempo markings are very imprecise at best, and were even more so prior to the invention of the metronome. This can be demonstrated by sampling four or five different recordings of a movement such as the "Allegro" finale of Bach's Brandenburg Concerto No. 3 in G Major, and comparing the tempos. Again, use of a metronome will underscore the differences.

Discussion Questions

1. The distinction between a musical tone and a noise was noted in Chapter 1. Are there any circumstances in which a noise might be a part of music?

2. We have seen that by clapping a rhythm we can have rhythm without melody. Can we also have melody without rhythm?

3. Given the information in Chapter 1, how can we sense that disjunct melodies tend to impart drama and energy, while conjunct melodies are capable of sweeter, more lyrical effects?

4. What do we mean when we say that any beat can be subdivided into either two or three units?

5. If two pieces of music are played at the same tempo, why is it possible for one to sound faster than the other?

Listening Questions

1. Suggested Example: Mozart, Symphony No. 40 in G Minor, K. 550, fourth movement, opening

   This movement from Mozart's Symphony No. 40 begins with a melody that is predominantly conjunct.
   True   *False

2. Suggested Example: Tchaikovsky, Symphony No. 6 in B

Minor, Op. 74 ("Pathétique"), second movement, opening

In this movement from his "Pathétique" Symphony,
Tchaikovsky used the unusual meter of $\frac{7}{4}$.
True   *False

3.   Suggested Example: Bach, <u>Prelude and Fugue in D Major</u>,
     BWV 532 ("Great"), fugue, opening subject statement

     A diagram of this melody by Bach would show a relatively
     quick ascent and a long, slow descent.
     *True   False

4.   Suggested Example: Dvořák, <u>Symphony No. 7 in D Minor</u>,
     Op. 70, third movement, opening

     In this example from Dvořák's <u>Seventh Symphony</u>, the rhythm
     of the melodic line remains rather static while the rhythm
     of the accompaniment fluctuates greatly.
     True   *False

5.   Suggested Example: Beethoven, <u>Symphony No. 3 in E^b Major</u>,
     Op. 55 ("Eroica"), first movement, opening

     The opening of Beethoven's "Eroica" Symphony features a
     passage of syncopated rhythm followed by a restatement of
     the first melody.
     *True   False

ANSWERS TO OBJECTIVE TEST (p. 105-06)

     1. d   2. b   3. c   4. a   5. c   6. d   7. a   8. b
     9. d   10. a   11. a   12. c   13. d   14. b   15. c
     16. b   17. a   18. c   19. b   20. d

ANSWERS TO COMPLETION TEST (p. 106-07)

     21. upward, downward   22. beginning, middle, end   23. art
     24. expressive   25. Italian   26. very fast, very slow
     27. very   28. smaller   29. rhythm   30. threes, twos

CHAPTER 2

HARMONY AND TEXTURE

Summary

Chapter 2 presents material intended to develop the students' awareness that harmony and texture create a musical depth and richness to the melodic and rhythmic lines. Just as disjunct and conjunct melodies create different feelings, so do different types of harmonies. The student should understand consonance and dissonance as well as recognizing and analyzing the three basic types of musical texture, monophony, homophony, and polyphony.

The following terms are introduced and should be understood by the student: interval, tonal center, chord, octave, chromatic, major and minor sclaes; tonic, dominant and subdominant triads; triad inversion; authentic and plagel cadences; accidentals, modulations, and the technique of arpeggiation.

Goals and Suggestions for Classroom Experiences

To understand the visual and aural perception of basic harmonic and textual musical sounds.

1. The richness that harmony adds to melody can be well illustrated with the opening movement of Schubert's Piano Sonata in B^b Major, D. 960. If the students first hear the melody unadorned, they will be able to observe that, however beautiful it is, it is somewhat static and lacking in drama. The octave doubling of the melody and the lavish harmonic support Schubert supplies throw the melody into a whole new perspective.

2. To demonstrate the fact that the octave is a different version of the same note, but pitched higher or lower, strike the F below middle C and ask the women in the class to duplicate it immediately. They will almost invariably produce the F an octave above the one actually played. The same demonstration may be given with the men by playing a note well above their normal vocal range.

3. The "more serious and somber" character of the minor mode is apparent in the third movement of Mahler's Symphony No. 1 in D Major, where the composer presents the "Frère Jacques" melody in the minor mode and constructs a sort of funeral march out of it. A class performance of the

4

round in its normal, major mode will make the contrast stand out even more starkly. Despite the ostinato bass and the added melodies, the students should have little difficulty in following the round in Mahler's setting.

4. The students should understand that contrapuntal techniques remain very much alive in the twentieth century. An example of a twentieth-century tour de force is the fugal first movement of Bartók's <u>Music for Strings, Percussion, and Celesta</u>. The work opens several possible areas of discussion, including chromaticism, dissonance, and the difference between imitative and nonimitative counterpoint.

5. All aspects of texture discussed in the chapter come together in Beethoven's <u>Fantasy for Piano, Chorus, and Orchestra</u>, Op. 80. The piano introduction is basically homophonic, with block chords, arpeggios, and scales, but there are prominent contrapuntal passages as well. Surprisingly, when the strings enter, the texture thins out to single monophonic melody, interrupted by homophonic piano passages. The main body of the work is homophonic with some polyphonic passages, including imitative counterpoint near the beginning.

Discussion Questions

1. How does harmony and texture add depth and richness to a piece of music?

2. As we listen to consonant and dissonant sounds, what can best describe them?

3. We have seen that the seventh step of the scale pushes strongly toward the tonic note. Does this give us any hint or is it merely a coincidence that the dominant chord contains the seventh scale step?

4. Throughout music history, textures have changed back and forth. Why do you feel that composers adhered to this practice?

5. The term "arpeggio" comes from the Italian word <u>arpa</u>, for harp. Why should the harp have given its name to arpeggiated chords?

Listening Questions

1. Suggested Example: Bach, <u>The Well-Tempered Clavier</u>, <u>Prelude No. 1 in C Major</u>, Book I

This prelude by Bach consists of chords that are
a. dissonant.   c. monophonic.
*b. arpeggiated.   d. polyphonic.

2. Suggested Example: Tchaikovsky, Symphony No. 2 in C Minor, Op. 17 ("Little Russian"), first movement, opening

After the opening chord of his Second Symphony, Tchaikovsky introduces the various textures in the following order:
a. homophonic, monophonic, polyphonic.
b. polyphonic, monophonic, homophonic.
c. monophonic, homophonic, polyphonic.
*d. monophonic, polyphonic, homophonic.

3. Suggested Example: Beethoven, Symphony No. 1 in C Major, Op. 21, fourth movement, opening

Beethoven begins the last movement of his First Symphony by gradually building up to a
*a. major scale.   c. chromatic scale.
b. minor scale.   d. dissonant chord.

4. Suggested Example: Stravinsky, Le Sacre du printemps, opening

The beginning of Stravinsky's Rite of Spring is
a. consonant and basically homophonic.
b. dissonant and basically homophonic.
c. consonant and basically polyphonic.
*d. dissonant and basically polyphonic.

5. Suggested Example: Brahms, Intermezzo in C# Minor, Op. 117, No. 3, opening

Which of the following elements is not present in the opening of this intermezzo by Brahms?
a. Basically conjunct melody
b. Use of the minor mode
*c. Triple meter
d. Basically monophonic texture

ANSWERS TO OBJECTIVE TEST (p. 108-110)

31. b   32. c   33. d   34. d   35. a   36. c   37. c   38. d
39. a   40. b   41. c   42. a   43. d   44. c   45. b
46. a   47. d   48. a   49. b   50. c

6

51. ninth 52. tonal 53. peaceful, stable 54. dissonance, consonance 55. major 56. modulation 57. monophonic 58. homophonic 59. two, more 60. harp

CHAPTER 3

TIMBRE AND DYNAMICS

Summary

Chapter 3 first explores timbre, focusing chiefly upon the types of voices and instruments that have developed within the Western musical tradition: their classification, ranges, and means of tonal production, including keyboard instruments such as harpsichord, clavichord, pipe organ and piano are also discussed. The subject of non-Western singing styles is also touched upon, though detailed treatment may be more appropriate in connection with Chapter 6. The combination of instruments into various ensembles and the evolution of the modern orchestra are considered next, along with the concomitant art of orchestration. The chapter concludes with a discussion of dynamics and a table of the common dynamic markings.

Goals and Suggestions for Classroom Experiences

1. The chapter's first sentence suggests an experiment. Classically trained artists have made numerous recordings of popular songs that may be compared with popular renditions of the same songs. Of even greater interest to the students, however, may be the 1976 album Classical Barbra (Columbia M 33452), if accessible. The album features Barbra Streisand singing various classical songs and arias. Again, comparisons should be instructive. Which versions do the students prefer in each instance? Why?

2. A similar comparison can be carried out to demonstrate the timbre of various individual instruments. If you can obtain Ralph Kirkpatrick's recording of Bach's Well-Tempered Clavier, Book I, on clavichord (Archive 2708 006), this would be an opportune time to fix the sounds of the clavichord, harpsichord, and piano in the students' minds. You may also want to use a recording of Book I of The Well-Tempered Clavier on organ (Arion 90622/3) to add to the comparison.

3. Music originally composed for piano can be virtually transubstantiated by a brilliant orchestrator. This can be illustrated by comparing Maurice Ravel's orchestral setting and Mussorgsky's Pictures at an Exhibition with the original piano setting. Claude Debussy's orchestration of Satie's Gymnopédies, Nos. 1 and 2 (originally Nos. 3 and 1, respectively) offers another possibility.

4. Mussorgsky's <u>Songs and Dances of Death</u> afford an opportunity to compare various orchestrations of the same work. Speculating that Mussorgsky intended to orchestrate the songs himself, various composers, including Rimsky-Korsakov, Glazunov, and Shostakovich, have undertaken the task. Several of these versions are available on records, as is an unattributed version "specially prepared" for the singer Kim Borg (Nonesuch 71215). Which orchestration do the students prefer? Why? Will anyone argue in favor of the original piano version?

5. Benjamin Britten's <u>A Young Person's Guide to the Orchestra</u> was expressly designed to illustrate the potential of the modern symphony orchestra. The work can be used to demonstrate virtually all aspects of instrumental timbre and dynamics. Equally effective in tying together both major elements of the chapter is Ravel's <u>Bolero</u>, which sustains interest almost entirely through the brilliance of its orchestration and a prolonged crescendo.

Discussion Questions

1. It has been stated that music is the "Univeral Language." How can people of many cultures identify with this concept?

2. There are tuned and non-tuned percussion instruments. How could you discuss the differences?

3. Just as the piano superceded the harpichord, how has electronic and computerized music superceded the piano?

4. Since there are no strings found in band music, which section plays the melody most often?

5. Since Italian is not considered the Univeral written language, why are most dynamic markings given in Italian?

Listening Questions

1. Suggested Example: Bartók, <u>Music for Strings, Percussion, and Celesta</u>, third movement, opening

   This excerpt from a work by Bartók uses all categories of instruments <u>except</u>
   a. chordophones.   c. idiophones.
   *b. aerophones.   d. membranophones.

2. Suggested Example: Beethoven, <u>Symphony No. 1 in C Major</u>, Op. 21, first movement opening

   Beethoven's <u>First Symphony</u> opens with two forte-piano

dynamic markings heard most clearly in the
a. violins.   c. percussion instruments.
b. string section.   *d. wind section.

3. Suggested Example: Brahms, <u>Serenade No. 2 in A Major</u>, Op.
    16, fifth movement, opening

    The orchestration of this serenade by Brahms is very
    unusual in that it contains <u>no</u>
    a. oboes.   *c. violins.
    b. clarinets.   d. strings.

4. Suggested Example: Sibelius, <u>Symphony No. 7 in C Major</u>,
    Op. 105, opening

    This symphony by Sibelius begins with a prominent
     a. diminuendo.   c. sforzando.
    *b. crescendo.   d. forte-piano.

5. Suggested Example: Beethoven, <u>Piano Sonata in C# Minor</u>,
    Op. 27, No. 2 ("Moonlight"), third movement, opening

    In this excerpt from the last movement of Beethoven's
    "Moonlight" Sonata, phrase endings are signaled by
    *a. sforzandos.   c. decrescendos.
     b. crescendos.   d. ritardandos.

ANSWERS TO OBJECTIVE TEST (p. 111-112)

    61. c   62. a   63. c   64. d   65. b   66. a   67. d   68. c
    69. a   70. d   71. b   72. b   73. c   74. d   75. a
    76. c   77. d   78. b   79. a   80. d

ANSWERS TO COMPLETION TEST (p. 113   )

    81. human voices 82. soprano 83. pizzicato 84. wood,
    metal 85. string, woodwind, brass, percussion 86. pipe
    organ 87. intensities 88. very soft 89. loud
    90. crescendo

CHAPTER 4

INTRODUCTION TO MUSICAL FORM AND STYLE

Summary

Chapter 4 is intended as an introduction to overall design or form in music, keeping in mind the fundamental principles of repetition and principle contrast. Detailed treatments of the larger concepts will be presented later in the text (e.g., sonata form, in Chapter 12). For now, it will suffice to introduce the students to the practice of outlining the formal articulations of a work by means of small and capital letters, to train them to perceive the overall structure of works in binary and ternary form, and to alert them to the possibilities of variation technique and the developmental procedures that will be a part of the larger forms. Brief mention is made of the types of compositions that can be constructed using the individual forms. The chapter concludes with a preliminary discussion of musical style, and a table listing the approximate dates of the various stylistic periods.

Goals and Suggestions for Classroom Experiences

1. The opening song, "Das Wandern," from Schubert's Die schöne Müllerin, D 795 is an excellent example of strophic song form. The students should understand that, while the music is repeated for each text stanza, it need not be repeated in exactly the same style every time but may change to fit the changing text. Particularly noteworthy in this song is the fourth stanza where the heavy millstones seem to "dance" in the music played in the piano's lower register.

2. Another example from Schubert's Die schöne Müllerin - No. 19, "Der Müller und der Bach" - can be used to illustrate ternary song form. In this case, the form (ABA) can be subdivided, since the first A section and the B section are both miniature ternary forms (aba).

3. The "Minuet" of Mozart's Symphony No. 40 in G Minor, K. 550 offers a good example of a large-scale ternary form. The diagram below can be used to illustrate the use of form in this particular movement. Modulations and areas of uncertain key are represented by diagonal broken lines. To sharpen the contrast between the A and B sections, labels and musical material in minor keys have been placed below the center line, with labels and material in major

keys above. <u>Formally</u> the sections are more alike than different, despite the changed mode, dynamics, and instrumentation.

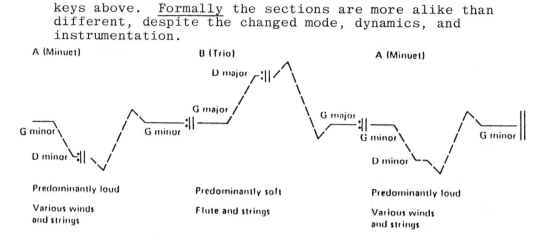

4. The dance movements from Bach's <u>English Suites</u> can be used as examples of binary form. The repetition of each of the two parts should, of course, be noted, along with examples of parallel construction between the parts. The harmonic goals of the two parts can be explained very simply - a modulation to a closely related key in the first part, and then a modulation back to the original key in the second part.

5. Mozart's <u>Variations on the Theme "Ah, vous dirai-je, Maman"</u>, K. 265 is a particularly useful example of theme and variations technique because of the students' familiarity with the theme. They should be able to follow is with little difficulty, as they observe the kinds of variation techniques brought into play. The eighth variation is especially interesting, showing the changed character of a familiar, "happy" tune when it is shifted to the minor mode.

<u>Discussion Questions</u>

1. How small can a motive be? How does a motive differ from a phrase?

2. What are some ways a composer can make use of repetition and contrast within form?

3. Can you think of some popular songs that are written in ternary form (ABA)?

4. How could you describe a movement in musical form?

5. Why do you suppose the dates given to the various stylistic periods are so imprecise?

Listening Questions

1. Suggested Example: Schubert, Die schöne Müllerin, D. 795, No. 16, "Die liebe Farbe"

   This song by Schubert is in ternary form.
   True   *False

2. Suggested Example: Bach, Orchestral Suite No. 2 in B Minor, "Badinerie"

   This movement by Bach is in binary form.
   *True   False

3. Suggested Example: Mahler, Des Knaben Wunderhorn, "Wer hat dies Liedlein erdacht"

   This song by Mahler is in strophic form.
   True   *False

4. Suggested Example: Schubert, Piano Sonata in G Major, D. 894, "Menuetto"

   This movement by Schubert is in ternary form.
   *True   False

5. Suggested Example: Stravinsky, Ebony Concerto, "Andante"

   This movement by Stravinsky is in ternary form.
   *True   False

ANSWERS TO OBJECTIVE TEST (p. 114-116)

   91. a   92. c   93. c   94. b   95. a   96. c   97. b   98. b
   99. b   100. b   101. d   102. c   103. b   104. a   105. c
   106. b   107. d   108. b   109. a   110. c

ANSWERS TO COMPLETION TEST (p. 116   )

   111. form 112. contrast, repetition 113. strophic 114. free
   form 115. lieder 116. rondo 117. symphonies
   118. eighteenth 119. section 120. seventeenth

CHAPTER 5

MUSICAL NOTATION

Summary

Chapter 5 provides the students with rudimentary data for reading and notating pitch, duration, and rhythm. A number of terms and concepts are presented, including ledger lines and clef placement; sharps, flats, and naturals; key signatures; relative major and minor scales; note values; ties, dots, and rests; bar lines; and meter signatures. The students should develop familiarity with the great staff and the common key signatures and meter signatures and the use of the metronome. In general, the students' main task will be to develop sufficient reading ability to enable them at least to follow the musical examples in the text.

Goals and Suggestions for Classroom Experiences

1. The students should realize that C clefs will occur in instrumental music as well as in vocal music. Indeed, the alto clef is often called the "viola clef." The score of Brahms' Piano Quintet in F Minor, Op. 34 juxtaposes traditional string quartet notation with the great staff of the piano, and thus can be used to expand the scope of the discussion of clefs and introduce the students to larger scores.

2. Erik Satie wrote much of his music with no indication of meter and without bar lines, even where the meter was quite obvious and regular. His Gnossienne No. 1 is a clear-cut example. Using an overhead projector, while listening to the piece, help the students supply the $\frac{4}{4}$ meter by placing bar lines in the appropriate spots.

3. Excellent examples of the typical use of common and cut time can be found in the opening movement of Beethoven's Piano Sonata in C Minor, Op. 13 ("Pathetique"), with alternating passages of each heard throughout the movement. A very atypical use of cut time in a slow movement occurs in the opening movement of Beethoven's Piano Sonata in C# Minor, Op. 27, No. 2 ("Moonlight"). Other movements of these two sonatas provide examples of $\frac{2}{4}$ and $\frac{3}{4}$ meter.

4. Using an overhead projector, have the students follow an example of a strophic hymn, and a popular piece in ABA form while listening to a recording of each type.

5. Demonstrate the use of the metronome by playing a section of a piece on the piano or a short recording while the metronome is keeping a steady tempo to the music.

Discussion Questions

1. Musical notation is designed to indicate what two things by using symbols?

2. What do the numbers of a meter signature indicate?

3. Since A# and B♭ share the same pitch or key on the piano, does it make any difference which symbol we use? Would it be incorrect to notate F major using a key signature of A# rather than B♭?

4. What is meant when we say that a major scale is paired with its relative minor?

5. Robert Schumann wrote that "you must reach the point where you can hear the music from the printed page"? Does this seem possible? Are only musical geniuses likely to attain this ability?

Listening Questions

1. Suggested Example: Beethoven, <u>String Quartet in F Major</u>, Op. 18, No. 1, first movement, <u>opening</u>

   This work by Beethoven can be most conveniently notated using two treble clefs, one alto clef, and one bass clef.
   *True   False

2. Suggested Example: Bach, <u>Sonata in B Minor for Flute and Harpsichord</u>, BWV 1030, first movement, opening

   This work by Bach can be most conveniently notated using the great staff and an additional bass clef.
   True   *False

3. Suggested Example: Dvořák, <u>Symphony No. 7 in D Minor</u>, Op. 70, first movement, opening - <u>not</u> including second theme

   The opening of this symphony by Dvořák, with one flat in its key signature, is in F major.
   True   *False

4. Suggested Example: Satie, <u>Gymnopédie No. 3</u>, opening

   If the time signature of this work by Satie is $\frac{3}{4}$, then

the smallest notes in the melody are probably quarter
notes.
*True   False

5. Suggested Example: Bach, <u>The Well-Tempered Clavier,
    Prelude No. 1 in C Major,</u> Book I

    If the bass notes in this prelude by Bach are half notes,
    then the high notes must be eighth notes.
    True   *False

ANSWERS TO OBJECTIVE TEST (p. 117-118)

   121. c 122. b 123. d 124. c 125. a 126. b 127. a 128. c
   129. b 130. c 131. d 132. a 133. d 134. b 135. c
   136. b 137. a 138. d 139. c 140. b

ANSWERS TO COMPLETION TEST (p. 118-119)

   141. staff 142. G 143. bass 144. half 145. rests
   146. bar lines 147. beats 148. natural 149. tie 150. slur

CHAPTER 6

MEDIEVAL MUSIC

Summary

Chapter 6 surveys the development of music from the early middle ages to the dawning of the Renaissance. Some cultural, social and political history is discussed, especially the Medieval Period, which lasted almost ten centuries with the feudal system and the Church remaining important throughout.

After briefly considering the general musical character-istics of the age, we find the vast majority of the music that survives from the Middle Ages is religious, since the Church was for many centuries the home of almost all learning. The chapter then takes up medieval religious music, in partic-ular, the Mass. The characteristics and notation of plain-chant and the characteristics and classification of modes are discussed in preparation for a detailed analysis of the Introit of the Requiem Mass. Finally, hymns are briefly considered.

Medieval secular music is discussed next, chiefly from the point of view of the French troubadours of the twelfth century. Bernart de Ventadorn's song, "Be m'an perdut," is discussed in detail. A discussion of the trouvères of Northern France was stated with a detailed listening analysis of "Li novious tens" by Le Châtelain de Coucy.

The chapter then goes on to treat Medieval polyphony. Following a general introduction, the work of the Notre Dame school is considered and exemplified by a discussion of Leonin's Viderunt omnes. The work of Perotin and the develop-ment of the motet are touched upon prior to the treatment of the next major topic, the Ars Nova of the fourteenth century. In this last section, Guillaume de Machaut and his virelai, "Douce dame jolie," are given special consideration. The chapter concludes with mention of the fourteenth-century poetic forms.

Goals and Suggestions for Classroom Experiences

1. For many centuries after the end of the Middle Ages, the Catholic Church continued to make extensive use of Gregorian chant, and most people had at least a passing familiarity with the style. Such familiarity can no longer be assumed. Some further investigation of the music is certainly in order, and a good many recordings are available for the purpose. A particularly interest-ing example is an Archive recording (3310 284) that contains examples of the generally more melismatic and

elaborate "Ambrosian" chant. These examples can be compared to the more typical chant style. How obvious are the stylistic differences to the untrained ear?

2. Adam de la Halle's Le Jeu de Robin et Marion is well worth hearing in its entirety. In addition to illustrating Medieval song style, unaccompanied and accompanied, it gives an introduction to the sound of the instruments of the period. Students should note the fine sense of restraint in the instrumentation.

3. Throughout the time spent on this chapter and the next, every effort should be made to familiarize students with the sound of early musical instruments. The Schwann catalogue lists numerous records devoted to early music. Particularly valuable for the purpose here are specialized collections, such as Vanguard's recording 71219-20 - Instruments of the Middle Ages and Renaissance.

4. Invaluable to the study of Medieval polyphony is the magnificent recent recording Music of the Gothic Era, produced by the late David Munrow (Archive 2723 045). This record set surveys the art of the Notre Dame composers, the ars antiqua, and the ars nova. Included is Perotin's Viderunt omnes, which can be profitably compared to Leonin's, discussed in the text. Note that Perotin replaces Leonin's virtuosic treatment of a single voice with an elaboration for several voices.

5. The recording mentioned in Suggestion 4 also features two examples of Philippe de Vitry's ars nova style, the motets "Impudenter circumivi" and "Cum statua." These should be heard with a particular view toward their rhythmic complexity. The set also contains ample material from the Ars Antiqua that can be used for comparison purposes.

Discussion Questions

1. Why was the Church so important in the development of music?

2. Why were instruments banned from the church of the Middle Ages?

3. Chants were generally built on one of eight modes or scales, do these modes still remain in use today?

4. Which parts of the Mass are best suited to a dramatic musical setting? Which parts are least suited?

5. Why was triple meter considered the "tempus perfectum"

in the Middle Ages? What is the mystical or religious significance of the number three?

Listening Questions

1. Suggested Example: Ventadorn, "Be m'an perdut," opening

   This is an example of Medieval secular music.
   *True   False

2. Suggested Example: Machaut, "Douce dame jolie"

   This is an example of Medieval homophonic texture.
   True   *False

3. Suggested Example: Requiem Mass, Dies irae, opening

   This example is from the Introit of the Requiem Mass.
   True   *False

4. Suggested Example: The Play of Daniel, "Ecce Rex Darius," opening

   This is an example of Medieval accompanied monophony.
   *True   False

5. Suggested Example: Leonin, Viderunt omnes, opening

   This is an example of parallel organum.
   True   *False

ANSWERS TO OBJECTIVE TEST (p. 120-122)

151. d 152. b 153. a 154. c 155. d 156. b 157. d 158. a
159. c 160. a 161. b 162. d 163. b 164. c 165. a
166. d 167. c 168. b 169. a 170. c

ANSWERS TO COMPLETION TEST (p. 122   )

171. ten 172. vesper 173. plaint chant 174. Notre Dame
175. perfect time 176. as one 177. proper, ordinary
178. ionian 179. neumatic, syllabic, melismatic
180. rhythmic

CHAPTER 7

RENAISSANCE MUSIC

Summary

Chapter 7 surveys the music of the Renaissance, beginning with a discussion of Renaissance style of life. The present life, rather than the afterlife was to become the focus of human outpouring. Education was freed from the confines of the church and the modern sciences of astronomy and anatomy began. As new techniques and instruments for navigating and mapping were developed, voyages by such men as Columbus, Vasco da Gama and Magellan were launched to explore new regions. Printing, using moveable type was invented. Individual creation was glorified, and the creative climate came to be known as humanism. Other events included the Hundred Years' War (1337-1453), Council of Trent (1545-1563), and loss of power and wealth by the church to merchants, princes and monarchs.

New musical styles evolved in the early fifteenth century as much of this century and the sixteenth century are thought as the Renaissance in music. The chapter continues with the general characteristics of Renaissance music such as singable melodies, use of counterpoint, four different voice parts, use of imitation, and harmony based on the Church modes. By the mid-Renaissance, four parts had become the normal number for a polyphonic work, resulting in fuller-sounding harmonies. There was a careful use of dissonance, mostly for special effect at the cadences. Words or phrases were often developed with Text Painting. Rhythms became more free with duple and triple meters combined in one piece.

Goals and Suggestions for Classroom Experiences

To understand imitative counterpoint as found in Renaissance Masses and motets.

To understand the differences between music for the Roman Catholic Mass and music for the Lutheran service.

To understand basic differences between Italian and Elizabethan madrigals.

1. Listening Summary for "Absalom fili mi" - Josquin (side 2, band 8)

    Timbre: small four-part unaccompanied choir

    Rhythm: duple meter

Harmony: based on Church mode

Texture: contrapuntal and imitative

Form: free, evolving from points of imitation and non-imitative counterpoint

2. Listening Summary for "Komm, Gott Schopfer heiliger Geist" - Johann Walter

This sacred composition which illustrates Reformation music of the Renaissance is found in A Treasury of Early Music, An Anthology of Masterworks; Volume 2, Music of the Ars Nova and Renaissance, Haydn Society Records.

Timbre: four-part unaccompanied choir

Rhythm: duple meter

Harmony: based on cantus fermus mode

Texture: imitative

Form: motet form, evolving from points of imitation

3. The diagram below may help to illustrate the rather free phrase structure of Monteverdi's madrigal "Si ch'io vorrei morire." Each phrase is represented by a horizontal or diagonal symbol representing its basic melodic contour - static, ascending, or descending. So that phrase repetitions can be recognized where they do occur, different phrases in a similar direction are represented successively by thin lines, bold lines, double lines, and triple lines. The opening phrase is repeated at the end, rounding out the structure. Other repetitions involve the f and g phrases in the second half of the work.

Phrases:

4. Compare the styles of Lassus and Gesualdo. Examples of Lassus' style may be found in the works "Matona mia cara" and "O la, o che bon' eccho" which are available in the Dover recording 97269-0. Compare these harmonies with the madrigal "Moro lasso" by Gesualdo which may be found in A Treasury of Early Music, An Anthology of Masterworks, Volume 3, Music of the Renaissance and Baroque, Haydn Society Records.

5. Listening Summary for "Now is the Month of Maying" - Morley (Side 2, Band 11)

    Timbre: five-part mixed vocal ensemble, unaccompanied

    Rhythm: duple meter

    Harmony: major scale

    Texture: homophonic

    Form: strophic, with each stanza in aabb form

6. Renaissance instrumental music can be explored with selections chosen from two excellent recordings: Musical Heritage Society's Gothic and Renaissance Dances (MHS 761) and Archive's Dance Music of the Renaissance (2533 111), The imprecision of Renaissance instrumentation can be observed by direct comparison of the several dances common to both collections. Not only does the instrumentation differ, but in some cases the formal arrangement of sections differs as well. Which arrangement of each work do the students like best?

Discussion Questions

1. What was the philosophical concept of humanism?

2. How did the Council of Trent influence the writing of Renaissance polyphony?

3. In what way did the relationship of music to words change during the Renaissance?

4. If the Renaissance musical style came early to Italy, what region or country was one of the latter ones to develop this style?

5. What was unique about the Venetian School as compared to the Roman School of Renaissance musical style?

Listening Questions

1. Suggested Example: Palestrina, Missa brevis, Kyrie, opening

    This is the opening of the Kyrie from Palestrina's Missa brevis.
    *True   False

2. Suggested Example: Morley, "My Bonny Lass"

This work is typical of an English Renaissance madrigal.
*True   False

3. Suggested Example: Gesualdo, "Moro lasso" (madrigal)
    opening

    To judge from its style, this madrigal is by Monteverdi.
    True   *False

4. Suggested Example: Morley, "Now is the Month of Maying"

    This work is written in five parts.
    *True   False

5. Suggested Example: Byrd, Mass for Five Voices, Kyrie,
    opening

    This work, by an English composer, is typical of the
    style of Dowland.
    True   *False

ANSWERS TO OBJECTIVE TEST (p.123-125)

   181. a 182. b 183. d 184. a 185. c 186. b 187. d 188. b
   189. c   190. d   191. a   192. b   193. c   194. a   195. d
   196. c   197. d   198. b   199. a   200. c

ANSWERS TO COMPLETION TEST (p. 125   )

   201. polyphonic 202. hymn 203. Lasses 204. antiphony
   205. humanism 206. Rome 207. Petrucci 208. madrigals
   209. fa-la-la   210. consorts

INTRODUCTION TO BAROQUE MUSICAL STYLES

Summary

Chapter 8 is designed as a brief description of the word Baroque and introduction to the Baroque era, with detailed treatment of the vocal and instrumental music of the period reserved for the two succeeding chapters. The chapter begins with a general discussion of the political, social, and artistic climate of the era, followed by the broad survey of the musical characteristics of the period. The instructor's concern, for now, is likely to be the clarification and illustration of the following technical concepts: monody, ornamentation, recitative and aria; Bel Canto Style, sequence, development of the major-minor system; chordal progression and modulation; the use of basso continuo and figured bass; the use of imitative counterpoint, instrumental timbre, beginning of the orchestra, terraced dynamics, and different types of Baroque compositions and form. The chapter concludes with a table comparing the specifics of Renaissance and Baroque music.

Goals and Suggestions for Classroom Experiences

1. In accordance with current notions of authenticity in performance, attempts have focused particularly on the areas of ornamentation and figured bass. An example of this trend is Raymond Leppard's recording of Bach's Orchestral Suites (Philips 839 792/3). One of the most controversial aspects of the recording is Leppard's elaborate ornamentation of the melody of the famous "Air" from Suite No. 3 by Bach.

2. A fine illustration of a very imaginative realization of a figured bass is Vittorio Negri's recording of Vivaldi's Four Seasons, Op. 8 (Philips 9500 100). Harpsichordist Jeffrey Tate does not confine himself to simple block chords, but, wherever possible, incorporates melodic activity into the figured bass. Note particularly the Largo of the Winter Concerto, where the harpsichord engages in imitative dialogue with the violin. The recording can very profitably be compared with other recordings employing a less imaginative realization of the figured bass.

3. The Fugue No. 8 in D# Minor from Bach's Well-Tempered Clavier, Book I, demonstrates many of the imitative

procedures used in fugal writing, including subject inversion, stretto, stretto in inversion, and rhythmic augmentation. The students should realize that this fugue is unusual in the intensive use of all these techniques, and particularly in its use of rhythmic augmentation.

Discussion Questions

1. What factors other than an interest in Greek drama might have been involved in the early Baroque movement away from complex vocal polyphony?

2. How can we explain the overt emotionalism found in much of Baroque art? Were these emotions present in Baroque music?

3. What effect did equal temperament have on Baroque keyboard music? What is a good example by J.S. Bach?

4. What was the make-up of the early Baroque orchestra?

5. Which is more important to the concertato style, competition, or collaboration? Are both implicit in the concertato style?

Listening Questions

1. Suggested Example: Bach, Magnificat in D Major, "Suscepit Israel"

   This movement by Bach clearly illustrates the early Baroque departure from the polyphonic vocal style of the Renaissance.
   True   *False

2. Suggested Example: Handel, Israel in Egypt, opening

   The brief orchestral introduction to this oratorio by Handel is basically homophonic.
   *True   False

3. Suggested Example: Manfredini, Concerto in D Major for Two Trumpets, first movement, opening

   In this concerto by Francesco Manfredini, the homophonic orchestral passage heard at the beginning is followed by the entrance of two trumpets in imitative counterpoint.
   True   *False

4. Suggested Example: Vivaldi, Autumn Concerto, first movement, opening

25

The opening of this concerto by Vivaldi presents a clear-cut example of terraced dynamics.
*True   False

5.   Suggested Example: Bach, <u>Cantata No. 140</u>, fourth movement, opening

The instrumental introduction of this movement from a Bach cantata consists of two melodic lines above a basso continuo.
True   *False

<u>ANSWERS TO OBJECTIVE TEST (p.126-127)</u>

211. b 212. c 213. a 214. d 215. c 216. d 217. a 218. b
219. d 220. c 221. b 222. a 223. b 224. a 225. d
226. c 227. c 228. b 229. d 230. a

<u>ANSWERS TO COMPLETION TEST (p. 128   )</u>

231. France 232. Doctrine of the affections 233. trill
234. flowing 235. altered 236. polyphony 237. musical
shorthand 238. oratorio 239. New England 240. Camerata

CHAPTER 9

BAROQUE VOCAL MUSIC

Summary

     Chapter 9 is a systematic survey of the most important
types of vocal music in the Baroque period: opera (Italian,
French, and English), the cantata (secular and sacred), the
oratorio, and the Mass. Detailed analysis is given to selections from Monteverdi's Orfeo, Bach's Cantata No. 80, Handel's
Messiah, and Bach's Mass in B minor. The chapter concludes
with a special listening exercise on the evolution of the
Mass.

Goals and Suggestions for Classroom Experiences

1. The recitative "Funeste piaggi," from Peri's Euridice
    (Historical Anthology of Music, No. 182) can serve as a
    test of Monteverdi's dictum: "The words should be the
    master, not the servant, of the music." To what extent
    is this ideal realized? Is the rhythm of the music com-
    patible with the natural rhythm of the Italian text? How
    does Peri paint particularly expressive words like
    "lampi," "dolenti," "chimè," "misero," and the like?

2. An opera written a year after Monteverdi's Orfeo, Marco
    da Gagliano's La Dafne (1608), illustrates just how
    advanced Monteverdi was in his instrumentation and in the
    overall conception of his opera. While Gagliano's writing
    shares many stylistic traits with Monteverdi's, Gagliano's
    score was so sketchy that performing versions have to be
    constructed for present day performances. The two avail
    able recordings (Archive 2533 348 and ABC 67012) offer the
    opportunity to compare two differing notions of early
    Baroque performance. Since the ABC version bases its
    instrumentation chiefly upon Monteverdi's score, some
    sections of Orfeo might be profitably also brought into
    the comparison.

3. Part I of Handel's Israel in Egypt provides a classic
    example of the Baroque fondness for text painting. The
    musical depictions of the various plagues visited upon the
    Egyptians display Handel's mature style in a diversity of
    textures and forms, including two recitatives and an aria
    amidst a variety of choruses. Despite the seriousness of
    the biblical text, the literalness of Handel's painting is
    not lacking in humor for the modern listener.

4. Bach's Cantata No. 78, "Jesu, der du meine Seele," is a fairly typical example of Bach's use of a chorale melody to open and close a cantata. If the students first hear the concluding chorale harmonization, they should quickly become familiar with the tune. They should then have little difficulty in recognizing the chorale tune in the opening fantasia as it appears periodically in the soprano voice, rhythmically altered and embellished. The basso ostinato that accompanies each successive phrase of the melody should also be pointed out. The second movement of the cantata, a duet in da capo form, features hurrying "footsteps" in the basso continuo, another example of text painting.

5. Bach's text painting often rises to the level of musical symbolism, as in the Saint Matthew Passion. In the early recitatives, an unmistakable string "halo" accompanies the words of Christ and distinguishes his portion of the recitative from that of the Evanglist. Note, however, the recitative near the end of the work, "Und von der sechsten Stunde an," where the halo no longer accompanies the words of Christ. The student with a taste for searching out text painting and musical symbolism should be encouraged to investigate Bach's Magnificat in D Major, where one will find both obvious and subtle examples.

Discussion Questions

1. What generally was the Baroque attitude toward texts? How clearly were the texts projected in the works you have heard? How extensive was textual painting?

2. In early Baroque opera what might have been the subject matter?

3. Monteverdi, in his opera Orfeo, made effective use of chromaticism, in what way?

4. Did the secular and sacred cantata differ in form?

5. Was Handel's compositional style most influenced by (a) his German upbringing, (b) his stay in Italy, or (c) his residence in England?

Listening Questions

1. Suggested Example: Bach, Cantata No. 3, "Ach Gott, wie manches Herzeleid," second movement

   This movement from a Bach cantata is best described as an alternation of phrases of

a. arias and recitativo secco.
b. arias and recitativo accompagnato.
*c. chorale harmonization and recitativo secco.
d. chorale harmonization and recitativo accompagnato.

2. Suggested Example: Monteverdi, Orfeo, "Tu se' morta"

    This selection from Monteverdi's Orfeo uses a basso
    continuo made up of organ and
    a. harpsichord.   c. viola da gamba.
    *b. lute.   d. cello.

3. Suggested Example: Handel, Messiah, tenor recitative,
    "Comfort Ye, My People"

    This movement from Handel's Messiah is best described as a
    a. strophic bass aria.   c. recitativo secco.
    b. da capo aria.   *d. recitativo accompagnato.

4. Suggested Example: Handel, Messiah, "Hallelujah" chorus

    This chorus from Handel's Messiah
    *a. is mainly homophonic, with some polyphonic passages.
    b. is mainly polyphonic, with some homophonic passages.
    c. contains about equal parts of homophony and polyphony.
    d. contains about equal parts of monophony, homophony,
        and polyphony.

5. Suggested Example: Bach, Mass in B Minor, Benedictus
    section of the Sanctus

    This selection from Bach's Mass in B Minor is the section
    of the Sanctus designated by the letter
    a. A.   c. C.
    b. B.   *d. D.

ANSWERS TO OBJECTIVE TEST (p. 129-131)

    241. a 242. b 243. d 244. a 245. c 246. a 247. c 248. b
    249. b 250. b 251. a 252. d 253. c 254. b 255. a
    256. b 257. d 258. c 259. a 260. b

ANSWERS TO COMPLETION TEST (p. 131)

    261. Monteverdi 262. vocal 263. Handel 264. Purcell
    265. Handel 266. Rossi 267. less important 268. Germany
    269. Lully 270. comic

29

CHAPTER 10

BAROQUE INSTRUMENTAL MUSIC

Summary

In the transition from Renaissance to Baroque style, vocal music was the medium which evolved most smoothly. The development of orchestras and the rise of instrumental music was, however, the single most important legacy of the Baroque era. Chapter 10 begins with a discussion of the emergence of the art of instrumentation and concomitant rise of the Baroque orchestra. It then treats the development of the chief instrumental compositions of the period: the sonata (trio, solo, and unaccompanied), the concerto (grosso and solo), and the fugue. The chapter ends with a brief discussion of the suite, the French and Italian overtures, the toccata, and the fantasia. Both ritornello and fugal forms are analyzed in depth, with graphic examples. Works singled out for detailed discussion are Scarlatti's Sonata in C Major K. 159, Vivaldi's Winter Concerto, Handel's Concerto in B♭ Major, Op. 3, No. 1, and Bach's Fugue in C Minor, BWV 578.

Goals and Suggestions for Classroom Experiences

1.   Giovanni Gabrieli's celebrated Sonata pian' e forte (Historical Anthology of Music, No. 173) can be used to illustrate several aspects of the developing Baroque instrumental style. This was one of the earliest works to specify loud and soft passages, opening the way to the Baroque practice of terraced dynamics. It was also unusual in its clear specification of instruments, a pioneering work in the art of instrumentation and thus in the development of the Baroque orchestra. The groups of instruments were stationed in various sections of the Basilica of Saint Mark's in Venice, and the resultant antiphonal effect was a forerunner of the Baroque concertato style. Passing mention can be made of the renewed interest in antiphonal effects by the avant-garde composers of our own day.

2.   Corelli's Sonata da chiesa in E Minor, Op.3, No. 7 (HSE 9040) can be used to illustrate the typical slow - fast - slow - fast order of movements. Also of interest in this trio sonata are the fugal style of the second movement and the dancelike quality of the last movement. Students should be able to identify the number and types of instruments involved in the work; in the HSE recording there are two violins, a cello, and an organ.

3. The following diagram may prove helpful in illustrating the use to the ritornello form in the two Baroque concertos discussed in the text. The first shows the opening movement of Vivaldi's Winter Concerto, the second the opening movement of Handel's Concerto in B^b Major, Op. 3, No. 1. In both diagrams, ritornello sections are represented by double lines, "solo" sections by single lines. The two groups of triple lines in the Vivaldi example illustrate an area of dialogue between solo and ripieno instruments and an area where the instruments are inextricably combined. Quick key changes are represented by changes in the height of the lines; areas of modulation are represented by broken lines. Students should be able to recognize both the similarities in the use of form in the two movements and the differences. Among the most prominent differences are those involving the treatment of modulation and key. Most of the key changes in the Vivaldi movements are rather abrupt, compared to the more deliberate modulations in the Handel movement. Handel's movement shows more variety in keys. You may also want to point out the unusual move to E^b major in the Vivaldi example; E^b major, the relative major of the dominant minor, will serve as the tonic of the second movement of the Vivaldi concerto.

Vivaldi:

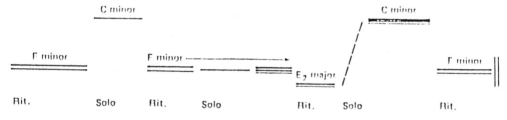

Handel:

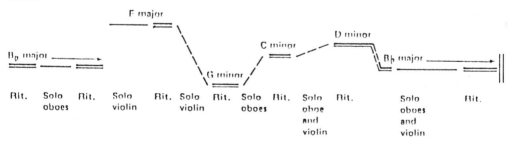

4. Two organ works by Bach, the Toccata and Fugue in D Minor, BWV 565 and the Passacaglia and Fugue in C Minor, BWV 582 can be used to further illustrate fugal techniques. The exposition of each fugue should be analyzed in some

detail, with subject entries and episodes noted. The improvisatory nature of the toccata and the variation technique exhibited in the passacaglia are also worthy of discussion.

5. Bach's <u>English Suite No. 3 in G Minor</u> can be used as an example of the expanded Baroque keyboard suite. The "Prelude" can be used to illustrate the importance of sequence in Baroque music. The dances - the "Allemande," "Courante," "Sarabande," and the two "Gavottes," and the concluding "Gigue" - can be studied in terms of their characteristic rhythmic patterns. A discussion of form should lead students to recognize the uniformly binary structure of the dances. Do students find any monotony in this uniformity of structure, or in the uniformity of tonality?

Discussion Questions

1. What factors account for the prominent of string instruments in Baroque orchestras, sonatas, and concertos?

2. One of the most important types of works for small orchestras to emerge during the seventeenth century was the concerto. What was unique about this genre?

3. Vivaldi liked programmatic music and often introduced what type of sounds?

4. Even though we have seen that the Baroque era developed longer, more complex forms, what accounts for the popularity of the suite?

5. What are some of the nonmusical factors that may account for the differences in the Italian and French overtures?

Listening Questions

1. Suggested Example: Bach, <u>Sonata for Flute and Basso Continuo in E Minor</u>, BWV 1034, second movement, opening

    This work by Bach could be best described as a
    a. trio sonata.
    b. sonata for flute and harpsichord.
    c. sonata for flute, violin, and harpsichord.
    *d. sonata for flute and basso continuo.

2. Suggested Example: Purcell, <u>The Married Beau</u> (Suite for String Orchestra), final movement, "Hornpipe on a Ground"

    This selection by Purcell would be most appropriate as

part of a(n)
a. concerto.
*b. suite.
c. overture.
d. sinfonia.

3. Suggested Example: Vivaldi, <u>Concerto for Two Oboes, Two Clarinets, and String Orchestra in C Major</u>, first movement, opening

In this concerto by Vivaldi, the concertino consists of
a. an oboe and two clarinets.
b. two oboes and a clarinet.
*c. two oboes and two clarinets.
d. three oboes and three clarinets.

4. Suggested Example: Bach, <u>A Musical Offering</u>, "Ricercare à 3," exposition

In this exposition of a fugue by Bach, the subject appears
a. twice.
*b. three times.
c. four times.
d. five times.

5. Suggested Example: Handel, <u>Water Music</u>, Suite No. 2, "Sarabande"

This movement from a Handel suite has the characteristics of a(n)
*a. sarabande.
b. gigue.
c. allemande.
d. overture.

ANSWERS TO OBJECTIVE TEST (p.132-134)

271. a 272. d 273. c 274. a 275. b 276. d 277. c 278. c
279. a 280. b 281. d 282. b 283. c 284. a 285. d
286. a 287. d 288. c 289. b 290. d

ANSWERS TO COMPLETION TEST (p. 134)

291. textural clarity, expressiveness 292. contrasting timbres 293. all 294. ritornello 295. opus 296. sequence
297. slow-fast 298. solo 299. dance 300. Frescobaldi

CHAPTER 11

INTRODUCTION TO THE MUSICAL STYLE OF THE CLASSICAL ERA

Summary

 Chapter 11, like previous introductory chapters, begins
with a discussion of the various cultural trends that shaped
the intellectual climate of the age. A section on the
emergence of the Classical style follows, with a consideration
of the largely negative reaction to Baroque music during the
period immediately following the death of Bach. It details
the elements of the Rococo style and of the so-called
Empfindsamer Stil, which marked the transition between the
Baroque era and the next great flowering of Western music in
the Classical period. Following a brief discussion of the
notion of a Classical-Romantic continuum, the main body of
the chapter considers the constituent elements of the Classical style: melody and theme, phrase structure, rhythm,
harmony, key signatures, major and minor modality, timbre and
dynamics, changes in texture and form. Composers began to
take advantage of the variety of instruments available, writing melodies with specific instruments in mind. They exploited tone color as a means of contrast more than had been done
before. Much attention was given to the matter of sonata
form. The chapter continues with an investigation of the
invention of the piano, types of compositions and forms, a
comparison chart of Baroque and Classical Style music, rondo
form, sonata-rondo form, binary form, ternary form, and theme
and variation form.
 Music in eighteenth century America with the singing
schools, William Billings, Lowell Mason, secular folk music,
European influence, Thomas Jefferson, Benjamin Franklin, and
Francis Hopkinson were discussed.

Goals and Suggestions for Classroom Experiences

1. Both Mozart and Beethoven freely acknowledged their debts
    to C.P.E. Bach, who was perhaps the most important link
    between the Baroque and Classical periods. A comparison
    of the pre-Classical style and the fully developed
    Classical style can be made using the concluding chorus,
    "Sicut erat in principio," of C.P.E. Bach's Magnificat,
    and the "Kyrie eleison" chorus of Mozart's Requiem K. 626.
    Mozart's work may have been influenced by Bach's for there
    are some similarities in the fugue subjects used in the
    two works, though Bach's is in D major and Mozart's in D
    minor. On the other hand, either subject, or both, may
    derive from the Fugue in A Minor from Volume II of J.S.

Bach's <u>Well-Tempered Clavier</u>. Whatever the relationship among the three works, they make for an instructive comparison. How strict is Mozart's fugal technique in comparison with C.P.E. Bach's? How does the fugal technique of either compare with J.S. Bach's? How does Mozart's instrumentation compare with C.P.E. Bach's? What is the dramatic import of each work?

2. The orchestra came to be somewhat larger and more standardized in instrumentation in the later eighteenth century. Although still small in comparison to nineteenth-century orchestras, it was capable of a wide variety of sounds and effects. Listen to the first movement of Haydn's <u>Symphony No. 94 in G Major</u> (side 4, band 1) and identify the principal groups of instruments that you hear. Observe any changes in the choice and use of instruments from the works of Bach, Handel, and Vivaldi in the early eighteenth century.

3. While improvisation itself began to wane in the Classical era, many pieces retained an improvisatory character. Mozart's <u>Fantasia in D Minor</u>, K. 397 for piano is an example. The students should attempt to identify those aspects of the work that contribute to its "fantasy" quality. The freely additive form can be pointed out, as well as the frequent changes of tempo, the vividly contrasting melodic materials, and the improvisatory cadenzas. The regular phrase structure and modulatory pattern of the lyrical D major allegretto section can be compared with the asymmetric patterns of the adagio passages and cadenzas.

4. Though rondo form was well developed by Haydn's time, he made use of a very ridumentary sort of rondo to conclude his <u>Symphony No. 96 in D Major</u> (the "Miracle"). Here there are no clear-cut contrasting themes, but merely "episodes" between recurrences of the main theme. Is it possible to trace the form with letter designations? How does this movement resemble the Baroque ritornello form? How does it differ?

Discussion Questions

1. In what senses was Classical music simpler than Baroque music? In what sense was it more complex?

2. Can a Baroque-Classical continuum be drawn up, with some composers leaning more toward the Baroque, and other toward the Classical style? Why is this difficult?

3. How do the characteristics of Classical music reflect the

aesthetic ideals of ancient Greek and Roman art?

4. Composers in the late eighteenth and early nineteenth
   centuries used the theme and variation form. What are
   the basic principles?

5. How did early musicians in eighteenth-century America
   parallel the lifestyle of Renaissance troubadors and
   trouvères?

Listening Questions

1. Suggested Example: C.P.E. Bach, Orchestral Symphony in
   G Major, first movement, opening

   The rhythmic quality of this movement by C.P.E. Bach is
   more Baroque than Classical.
   *True   False

2. Suggested Example: Mozart, Adagio and Fugue in C Minor
   for String Orchestra, K. 546, fugue, opening

   This fugue by Mozart differs from Baroque fugues in that
   it becomes homophonic after the exposition.
   True   *False

3. Suggested Example: Haydn, Concerto No. 1 in C Major for
   Organ and Orchestra, last movement

   This movement from a Haydn organ concerto is more Baroque
   in form than Classical.
   True   *False

4. Suggested Example: Mozart, Piano Concerto No. 20 in D
   Minor, K. 466, first movement, opening

   In this movement from a Mozart piano concerto, the key
   relationship of first and second themes is minor mode/
   relative major.
   *True   False

5. Suggested Example: Beethoven, String Quartet in C Minor,
   Op. 18, No. 4, last movement

   The rondo form of this movement from a Beethoven string
   quartet can be diagramed ABACABA.
   *True   False

ANSWERS TO OBJECTIVE TEST (p. 135-137)

301. a 302. b 303. d 304. b 305. d 306. a 307. b 308. c
309. a 310. d 311. d 312. b 313. a 314. d 315. b
316. c 317. c 318. a 319. b 320. c

ANSWERS TO COMPLETION TEST (p. 137)

321. age of revolution 322. order, symmetry 323. linear
324. phrases 325. Classical 326. homophonic, less complex
327. string 328. Italy 329. ABACA 330. America

CHAPTER 12

SYMPHONIES OF HAYDN AND MOZART

Summary

Chapter 12 deals with the musical style of the symphonies of Haydn and Mozart. It also provides some biographical details about the two composers and background material on aristocratic patronage of artists in the eighteenth century and the late eighteenth-century rise of the modern public concert system. Two works are treated in great detail: Haydn's Symphony No. 94 in G Major (the "Surprise"), and Mozart's Symphony No. 40 in G Minor, K. 550.

Goals and Suggestions for Classroom Experiences

1. The following diagram can be used to illustrate two simple examples of Classical sonata forms, the first movements of the two symphonies discussed in the text: Haydn's Symphony No. 94 in G Major and Mozart's Symphony No. 40 in G Minor. Quick key shifts are represented by changes in the height of the lines; areas of modulation and uncertain keys are represented by broken lines. Students should be able to see the basic similarities in the two movements and the most obvious differences: the presence of an introduction in the Haydn example and the modulation to the relative major rather than the dominant in the Mozart example. More subtle differences can also be found, including the proportionately longer closing sections in the Mozart movement.

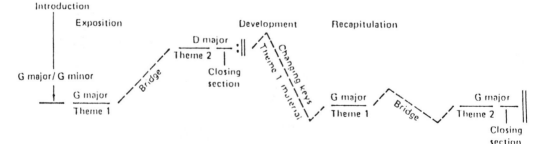

Mozart:

Exposition   Development   Recapitulation

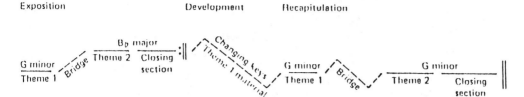

2. One of Haydn's earlier symphonies, a symphony such as the
   Symphony No. 44 in E Minor (the "Trauer-Symphonie"), can
   be used to provide an interesting comparison with the
   mature "Surprise" Symphony. Among the striking techniques that can be noted in the "Trauer-Symphonie" are
   the strict canons at the octave in the Minuet and, in the
   last movement, the long, rising sequences at the beginning of the development section, which are used to create
   great intensity.

3. Mozart's last symphony, the Symphony No. 41 in C Major,
   K. 551 (the "Jupiter") may be considered in some detail.
   The first movement, in sonata form, can be discussed with
   the usual eye toward developmental procedures and the
   overall modulatory plan. A peculiarity of the second
   movement worthy of particular note is the fact that the
   strings are muted. Do the students have any thoughts as
   to why the composer might have requested the use of
   mutes? The last movement is, of course, extremely complex. Particular attention should be paid to the famous
   passages in invertible counterpoint in the development
   section and coda. How do the students react to this
   movement? Do they have any thoughts as to how the
   symphony's subtitle might have come about?

Discussion Questions

1. How does Haydn's relationship to his patrons, the
   Esterházys, compare to the relationships between musician
   and Church in the Middle Ages, composer and court in the
   Renaissance, and composer and university in the twentieth
   century?

2. What does it mean to speak of the "mature" style of
   Mozart, who died at age 35? What indications are there
   in his late symphonies of the directions he might have
   pursued had he lived longer?

3. Both Haydn and Mozart are regarded as "Classical" composers, and their lives touched at various points. Many
   experienced listeners, however, can immediately distinguish the music of one composer from that of the other.

On the basis of what you have heard so far, can you pinpoint those features of their respective styles that make
them distinctive?

4. Many people consider the symphony the pinnacle of Western
    musical development. What historical tendencies converged
    to make up the symphony? What were the prerequisites to
    the development of the symphony in the realm of harmony?
    form? texture? instrumental development and instrument-
    ation?

5. It has been said that all great music is "Romantic" at its
    moment of conception. What does this provocative remark
    mean to you? What does it imply about music of the
    Classical era? Is the statement valid?

Listening Questions

1. Suggested Example: Haydn, <u>Symphony No. 94 in G Major</u>,
    second movement, opening

    This movement from Haydn's <u>Symphony No. 94 in G Major</u> is
    in
    a. sonata form.   *c. theme and variations form.
    b. Sonata-rondo form.   d. rondo form.

2. Suggested Example: Mozart, <u>Symphony No. 29 in A Major</u>,
    K. 201, first movement, opening

    In this sonata-form movement by Mozart, imitative counter-
    point signals the start of the
    a. first theme.   c. second theme.
    *b. bridge passage.   d. development.

3. Suggested Example: Haydn, <u>Symphony No. 100 in G Major</u>
    (the "Military"), second movement, opening through entry
    of percussion instruments

    This movement, in some ways very similar to one you have
    previously heard, is by
    *a. Haydn.   b. Mozart.

4. Suggested Example: Mozart, <u>Symphony No. 40 in G Minor</u>,
    K. 550, last movement, opening

    This movement from Mozart's <u>Symphony No. 40 in G Minor</u>,
    is in
    *a. sonata form.   c. theme and variations form.
    b. sonata-rondo form.   d. rondo form.

5. Suggested Example: Mozart, <u>Symphony No. 39 in E^b Major</u>,

K. 543, last movement, opening

An unusual feature of this movement by Mozart is that
a. the bridge passage in the exposition does not include
    modulation.
b. the bridge passage in the exposition includes a dis-
    tinctive new theme.
c. there is no second theme.
*d. the second theme is a variant of the first.

ANSWERS TO OBJECTIVE TEST (p. 138-140)

331. b 332. d 333. c 334. b 335. a 336. c 337. d 338. b
339. a 340. c 341. d 342. a 343. d 344. b 345. a
346. d 347. c 348. d 349. b 350. a

ANSWERS TO COMPLETION TEST (p. 140)

351. four 352. Haydn 353. Haydn 354. theme, variations
355. middle-class 356. Haydn, Mozart 357. Jupiter
358. Fidelio 359. Beethoven 360. chorus, soloists

CHAPTER 13

SYMPHONIES OF BEETHOVEN

Summary

Chapter 13 begins with a discussion of Beethoven's life
and the turbulent times within which he produced many of his
greatest works - the years of the French Revolution, the
Reign of Terror, and the Napoleonic Wars. For stylistic
reasons Beethoven's compositions are often classified as
belonging to his "early," "middle," or "late" period.
His first two symphonies are early works: Nos. 3-8 are
from his middle period (1802-1814), and the Ninth Symphony is
a major work from his late period. Several piano sonatas,
three piano concertos, and a set of string quartets are also
early works. Into his middle period fall his only opera,
Fidelio (1803), more string quartets and piano sonatas,
overtures, incidental music, a violin concerto, and two more
remarkable piano concertos. One gigantic work stands beside
the Ninth Symphony in his final period: the Missa solemnis
in D Major (1823), a setting of the Mass which Beethoven himself regarded as his finest work. It contains some of the
hardest choral music ever written, and, like the Ninth
Symphony, is a statement of universal faith. After these
enormous works, Beethoven returned to the smaller form of the
string quartet. His final compositions of this type are
unrivalled in their powerful and personal expressiveness.
The remainder of the chapter is devoted to a thorough discussion of his Symphony No. 5 in C Minor, Op. 67.

Goals and Suggestions for Classroom Experiences

1. Beethoven's Symphony No. 5 in C Minor contains two movements in sonata form, the first and the last. Both are
   outlined below following the style used for earlier
   diagrams in the manual. The similarities in the two
   movements are obvious, but students should also be able to
   note certain differences. The first movement, in the
   minor mode, modulates first the the relative major, while
   the last movement, in the major mode, modulates to the
   dominant. The development section is proportionately
   longer in the finale, and the coda is very lengthy - in
   effect, it is a coda to the entire symphony. Both movements can profitably be compared to the Haydn and Mozart
   movements diagramed in Chapter 12 of the manual. Such a
   comparison should help students see the extent to which
   Beethoven expanded the development section and coda of
   the Classical form. It should also be noted that
   Beethoven's bridge modulations are more abrupt than those

of the earlier composers.

First Movement:

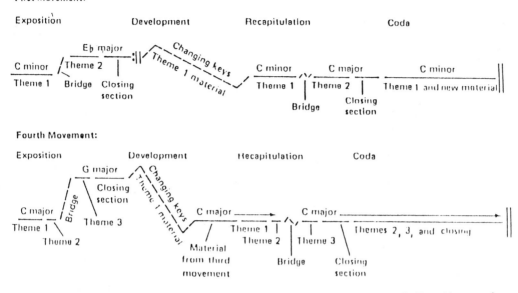

Fourth Movement:

2.   Diagrams of the second and third movements of Beethoven's
     Symphony No. 5 in C Minor may also merit extended class-
     room discussion. Among the points that can be mentioned
     in the second movement is the A^b major/C major juxta-
     position, a departure from traditional harmonic practice
     in the key relationships of thirds that certain Romantic
     composers, notably Brahms, later used so effectively. The
     ternary form of the third movement is so complex and
     varied, and can profitably be compared to the diagram of
     the Mozart Minuet (Symphony No. 40 in G Minor) found in
     Chapter 4 of the manual.

Second Movement:

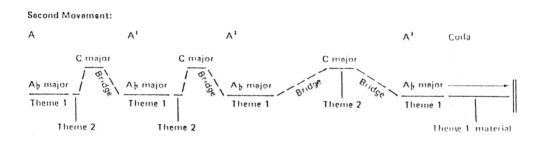

43

Third Movement:

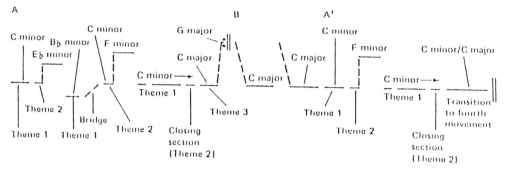

3. As inevitable as Beethoven's great symphonic themes sound, at least one of them had a rather modest origin. A very close model of the first theme of Beethoven's Symphony No. 3 in E♭ Major, Op. 55 (the "Eroica") can be found in the overture to Mozart's miniature opera, Bastien et Bastienne, K. 50. The students should realize that, in Beethoven's time, no stigma was attached to such borrowing. It was common, and, far from being regarded as plagiarism, was seen as a mark of respect toward the earlier composer. Beethoven showed no less creativity in totally transforming Mozart's relatively simple theme than he could have shown with an original melody.

4. The enormous growth of Beethoven's expressive power and mastery of form can be well demonstrated by juxtaposing the opening movements of his Symphony No. 1 in C Major, Op. 21 and Symphony No. 9 in D Minor, Op. 125. Every aspect of the sonata form is vastly extended in the latter work, resulting in the longest single movement created up to that time. The contrast between the finales, of course, is even starker. Two movements could hardly be more unlike than the sonata form that ends the First Symphony and the vast choral finale of the Ninth Symphony.

5. At this point, the first movement of Beethoven's Symphony No. 8 in F Major, Op. 93 may offer an interesting departure. On the basis of what they have heard of the Fifth and Ninth Symphonies, how do the students react to the symphony that preceded the Ninth? Many critics have seen the symphony as a regression of sorts. After having produced a series of grandiose symphonies, Beethoven scaled this symphony down to the trim proportions of his First Symphony. We, of course, are in a position to know what was to follow, and so we know that his powers were not failing and that he certainly was not becoming conservative. How might we have reacted at the time? Why did Beethoven reverse himself in this manner? What is the stature of this work among his other symphonies?

Discussion Questions

1. It is often said that Haydn's music has its roots in the peasant traditions of his native land. Do you find similar folk elements in any of the Beethoven symphonies that you have encountered?

2. The end of Beethoven's Fifth Symphony, with its endless repetitions of the C major triad, has offended many listeners from the day it was first performed to the present. What is the justification for this ending?

3. To what extent do you think Beethoven's character and personality were shaped by the social and political events of his time?

4. Just how Classical was Beethoven? how Romantic?

5. Beethoven's career helped introduce the concept of "artist as hero" into the history of Western music. Does this idea seem at all reasonable today, in an age when people have walked on the moon and created life in test tubes? How do you think Bach would have reacted to the idea?

Listening Questions

1. Suggested Example: Beethoven, <u>Symphony No. 1 in C Major</u>, Op. 21, first movement, opening

    This movement is part of one of Beethoven's
    *a. earliest symphonies.   c. most programmatic works.
     b. last symphonies.   d. Fifth Symphony.

2. Suggested Example: Beethoven, <u>Symphony No. 5 in C Minor</u>, third movement, opening

    This movement is in what form?
    *a. ABA   c. Rondo
     b. Theme and variations   d. Sonata

3. Suggested Example: Beethoven, <u>Symphony No. 5 in C Minor</u>, fourth movement, opening

    An unusual feature of this movement is the presence of
     a. voices.   c. a tuba.
    *b. a piccolo.   d. a bass drum.

4. Suggested Example: Beethoven, <u>Symphony No. 9 in D Minor</u>, Op. 125, last movement, introduction

    Which of the following is <u>not</u> a characteristic of the

introduction to the last movement of Beethoven's Ninth
Symphony?
a.   High strings playing a very minor role
b.   Monophonic interruptions in the low strings
c.   A great variety of themes
*d.   Steady tempo and constant meter

5.   Suggested Example: Beethoven, Symphony No. 9 in D Minor,
second movement, opening

Despite its unusual location in the work, the second movement of Beethoven's Ninth Symphony is a clear-cut example
of a
a.   choral movement.   c.   rondo.
*b.   scherzo.   d.   theme and variations form.

ANSWERS TO OBJECTIVE TEST (p. 141-143)

361. d 362. c 363. b 364. d 365. a 366. b 367. c 368. b
369. a 370. c 371. a 372. b 373. d 374. c 375. a
376. b 377. d 378. a 379. b 380. a

ANSWERS TO COMPLETION TEST (p. 143   )

381. Beethoven 382. French Revolution 383. fifth 384. nine
385. early, middle, late 386. Ode to Joy 387. vocal
388. Haydn, Beethoven 389. sixth   390. deafness

CHAPTER 14

CONCERTOS OF MOZART AND HIS CONTEMPORARIES

Summary

Chapter 14 begins by tracing the development of the Classical concerto to its origins in the Baroque concerto grosso and solo concerto. Also noted is the influence of Italian opera upon the Classical concerto and upon the Classical style in general. The mechanics and structure of the concerto are then discussed, with particular attention to the solo-orchestra relationship, the cadenza, and the adaptation of the sonata form to include the customary double exposition. Following a brief discussion of Mozart's concerto output, a detailed examination of his Piano Concerto No. 17 in G Major, K. 453 is undertaken. The chapter concludes with a brief survey of the concertos of Haydn and Beethoven.

Goals and Suggestions for Classroom Experiences

1. The diagram below, of the first movement of Mozart's Piano Concerto No. 17 in G Major, can be used to illustrate the adaptation of the sonata form to accommodate the solo instrument in a concerto. Comparison with the Mozart symphony movement diagramed in Chapter 13 of the manual will illustrate the added complexity that arises with the addition of a second, altered exposition and a new theme. Despite the added complexity, the only really surprising element in the diagram is the recurrence of the second theme in the closing section of the solo exposition.

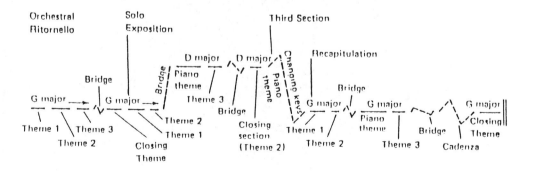

2. An excellent example of Haydn's concerto style is the Concerto for Trumpet and Orchestra in E^b Major. The

orchestration is comparable to that of his late symphonies. Haydn was fond of music with a military cast, which may help to explain his prominent use of the timpani in conjunction with the trumpet in the first and third movements. Many Baroque trumpet concertos left the trumpet out of the slow movement, due to the difficulty of performing quiet, lyrical melodies on that instrument. Do the students agree that Haydn has effectively surmounted that problem in his slow movement?

3. The first movement of Beethoven's Piano Concerto No. 4 in G Major, Op. 58 offers several avenues for discussion. One arises immediately: What are those five measures of solo piano music doing before the formal start of the exposition?

Discussion Questions

1. How can an instrument such as a clarinet or a violin compete on equal terms with a symphony orchestra? Why does it take a virtuoso performer to do so?

2. How does the concerto contrast the soloist and the orchestra?

3. Mozart and Beethoven were famous for their ability to improvise cadenzas to their concertos. Is it reasonable to assume that these cadenzas were created on stage, entirely on the spur of the moment?

4. How can the Classical-Romantic continuum be seen in Beethoven's concertos?

5. If you were about to hear Beethoven's Piano Concerto No. 4 played by a young virtuoso, would you rather hear the cadenzas written by Beethoven, or new ones created by the soloist?

Listening Questions

1. Suggested Example: Mozart, Concerto in C Major for Flute and Harp, K. 299, third movement, opening through second exposition

   This movement is part of a Mozart concerto for flute and harpsichord.
   True   *False

2. Suggested Example: Beethoven, Concerto in C Major for Violin, Cello, and Piano, Op. 56 (the "Triple"), last movement, opening

This is a movement from a concerto by Haydn.
True   *False

3. Suggested Example: Mozart, <u>Piano Concerto No. 17 in G</u>
    <u>Major</u>, third movement, opening

    This movement from Mozart's <u>Piano Concerto No 17 in G</u>
    <u>Major</u> is in theme and variations form.
    *True   False

4. Suggested Example: Mozart, <u>Piano Concerto No. 17 in G</u>
    <u>Major</u>, second movement, opening

    This second movement from Mozart's <u>Piano Concerto No. 17</u>
    <u>in G Major</u> begins in the major mode.
    *True   False

5. Suggested Example: Beethoven, <u>Piano Concerto No. 5 in E^b</u>,
    Op. 73 (the "Emperor"), first movement, opening

    The opening of Beethoven's "Emperor" Concerto is typical
    of the Classical concerto opening.
    True   *False

<u>ANSWERS TO OBJECTIVE TEST (p. 144-146)</u>

   391. b 392. d 393. b 394. a 395. a 396. a 397. d 398. b
   399. c 400. d 401. b 402. a 403. c 404. d 405. a
   406. c 407. b 408. a 409. d 410. c

<u>ANSWERS TO COMPLETION TEST (p.146   )</u>

   411. musical interplay 412. violin 413. opera 414. three
   415. elaboration 416. harpsichord, violin 417. orchestra
   418. fast, slow, fast 419. orchestra 420. solo

CHAPTER 15

CHAMBER MUSIC OF HAYDN, MOZART, AND BEETHOVEN

Summary

Chamber music, or <u>Hausmusik</u>, as it was appropriately referred to in the eighteenth century is defined in Chapter 15 as music composed for a small, conductorless group of performers, with only one player to a part. The small scale of the performing force permits a very personal, intimate expression. The similarities and differences between the symphony and the string quartet are not surprising when we consider the history of both compositional forms. We find that through Haydn, the string quartet, the most important type of Classical chamber music, took definite form. Although other types of chamber music are mentioned, interest is centered on the string quartet and the piano sonata. The classical sonata is traced from its origin in the Baroque era to its culmination in the works of Haydn, Mozart, Beethoven, and Schubert, and its structure is analyzed. Two works are treated in detail: Haydn's <u>String Quartet in C Major</u>, Op. 76, No. 3 ("Emperor") and Beethoven's <u>Piano Sonata in C Minor</u>, Op. 13 ("Pathetique").

There is an evolution of keyboard music chart which includes works from the Baroque, Classical/Romantic, Romantic and Modern.

Goals and Suggestions for Classroom Experiences

1. An excellent representative of Beethoven's early quartets is his <u>Quartet in F Major</u>, Op. 18, No. 1. The first movement, in particular, may be profitably analyzed. Note the incredible exploitation of the six-note motive with which the work opens. A useful comparison can be made with a later work. Of all the marvels among the last of Beethoven's quartets, perhaps none is more astonishing, or more "contemporary" in its implications, than the torrential <u>Grosse Fugue in B^b Major</u>, Op. 133. The structure of the whole work is predicated upon the material exposed in the first page of the score.

2. A Classical chamber work of a wholly different sort is Mozart's <u>Quintet in E^b Major</u>, K. 452, for piano and winds. To what extent does this work reflect the chamber style we have seen in the quartets? Is each of the wind instruments treated individually, or are the winds more often treated as a group? There are at least some elements of concerto style at work here. To what extent does the work resemble the concertos discussed in Chapter 15?

3. A fascinating example of Schubert's piano style is found in <u>Sonata in G Major</u>, D. 894. The first movement, in particular, merits analysis. Few sonata forms have been built on so static a first theme. But note the breadth of motion Schubert achieves and the harmonic interest he establishes around the theme. This sonata is often called a "Fantasia." What justification is there for such a title?

Discussion Questions

1. To what extent is a string quartet merely a scaled-down symphony? Is the only difference in orchestration and timbre, or is there a more fundamental difference in mode of expression?

2. The string quartet is regarded by many listeners and composers as the ideal string medium. What might be the reason for this thinking?

3. Can you state some differences between Beethoven's early and late chamber works?

4. Many of the early string quartets were called <u>divertimenti</u>. What does that mean?

5. Schubert's best known chamber work is the <u>Piano Quintet in A Major</u> ("the trout"). It is written for violin, viola, cello, and string bass. What is unusual about this combination of instruments?

Listening Questions

1. Suggested Example: Beethoven, <u>Piano Trio in B♭ Major</u>, Op. 97 (the "Archduke"), first movement, opening

   This work be Beethoven would be best described as a
   a. trio sonata.   *c. piano trio.
   b. string trio.   d. piano quartet.

2. Suggested Example: Beethoven, "Pathétique" Sonata, second movement, opening

   Beethoven's tempo marking for this movement of his "Pathétique" Sonata is
   a. Presto.   c. Allegro molto.
   b. Andante, poco agitato. *d. Adagio cantabile.

3. Suggested Example: Mozart, <u>Quintet in E♭ Major</u>, K. 452 (piano and winds), first movement, opening

This work by Mozart for piano and winds is a
a. trio.   *c. quintet.
b. quartet.   d. sextet.

4. Suggested Example: Beethoven, <u>String Quartet No. 7 in F
    Major</u>, first movement, opening

    The meter of this movement is
    *a. duple.   c. irregular.
    b. triple.   d. always changing.

5. Suggested Example: Beethoven, <u>String Quartet No. 14 in C
    Minor</u>, Op. 131, first movement, opening

    This string quartet was written by
    a. Haydn.   *c. Beethoven.
    b. Mozart.

ANSWERS TO OBJECTIVE TEST (p.147-149)

   421. c 422. b 423. c 424. b 425. b 426. a 427. d 428. b
   429. c 430. b 431. b 432. c 433. b 434. a 435. c
   436. c 437. b 438. a 439. b 440. b

ANSWERS TO COMPLETION TEST (p. 149)

   441. small 442. string quartet 443. piano 444. clear,
   transparent 445. divertimenti 446. Emperor 447. The Trout
   448. minuet 449. Franz Schubert 450. "Appassionata"

CHAPTER 16

VOCAL MUSIC OF THE LATE EIGHTEENTH CENTURY

Summary

   In Chapter 16, the focus is on opera, although the other
major vocal forms of the classical period - oratorio and the
Mass - receive some treatment. The nature of opera is defined, and its conventions are explained through analogy to
conventions in the visual arts and drama. Various categories
of operatic voices, male and female, are described, as are the
makeup and function of ensembles and choruses and their dis-
tribution through the opera according to the varying demands
of the libretto. The role of the orchestra is explained, as
well as the importance of opera's visual elements, the scenery
and staging.
   As vital as the singers and orchestra to opera perform-
ance are the conductor and stage director. The conductor
balances the orchestral and vocal forces and coordinates the
orchestra (which cannot hear or see much on-stage action) with
the singers. Molding the singers' different interpretations
into a musical whole is another aspect of the conductor's
role. The stage director ensures that the opera is theatri-
cally plausible and that the meaning of the music is projected
through the stage action.

Goals and Suggestions for Classroom Experiences

1.   The students may benefit from some exposure to the infre-
     quently heard music of Gluck. His opera Orfeo ed Euridice
     is a fine example. The contrasting scenes of Act II pro-
     vide excellent material, though time may not permit hear-
     ing both scenes in their entirety. The first scene con-
     tains the choruses and dances of the Furies attempting to
     bar Orfeo's way to the land of the dead. Note the in-
     creasing vehemence of the successive choruses throughout
     the scene, as Orfeo nears his goal. The contrast between
     this scene and the next, in the company of the Blessed
     Spirits in Elysium, could hardly be more stark. How do
     the students react to Gluck's rather formal style? Do
     they find it more pleasing than Mozart's, or less so?

2.   A single duet from Fidelio will suffice to show that
     Beethoven carried into opera the same musical dynamism
     that distinguished his instrumental music. Some critics
     content, in fact, that that was his problem in opera. The
     Act II duet between Leonora and Florestan, "O namenlose
     Freude," is in simple ternary form with some harmonic

complexities. But what should be noted are the nature of the melody and the orchestration. The opening melody is nothing less than a "Mannheim rocket," the musical device that Classical composers so enjoyed using in their symphonies.

4.   While the emphasis in this chapter has been placed on opera, other vocal music of the Classical period should be examined, if time allows. Mozart's Requiem offers a good example, since it afford a means of contrasting Mozart's sacred style with that of his operas. In the opening section of the Requiem, note the alternating use of strict imitation and homophony and the key changes. The Kyrie section offers a chance to introduce the concept of "double fugue," a fugue having a double subject, or two coordinating subjects.

5.   To compare the "sacred" styles of the various Classical composers, the Kyrie of Mozart's Requiem can be contrasted with the corresponding movements of Haydn's "Lord Nelson" Mass and Beethoven's Missa solemnis. How does each composer strike the balance between polyphony and homophony?

Discussion Questions

1.   Why should works connected with Church services and works with biblical texts have been less popular than opera in the Classical era? What was the standing of the church in that age?

2.   What alterations have to be made in a play to turn it into an operatic libretto?

3.   Can poor music survive on the basis of a good libretto? Conversely, can a poor libretto survive on the basis of good music?

4.   To what extent was Mozart's Marriage of Figaro a satirical commentary on the social structure of his time?

5.   Why wasn't Beethoven a more prolific operatic composer?

Listening Questions

Suggested Example: Mozart, The Marriage of Figaro, Act I

1.   In the first duet from The Marriage of Figaro, Figaro does his measuring in a triple meter.
     True   *False

2.   The recitative that follows is a duet in recitativo secco.

54

*True   False

3. In the next duet, the basic major key is offset briefly
    by the relative minor.
    *True   False

4. The recitative that follows begins as a duet in recita-
    tivo secco and then turns into a duet in recitativo
    accompagnato.
    True   *False

5. Figaro's next number is called a cavatina.
    *True   False

ANSWERS TO OBJECTIVE TEST (p. 150-151)

   451. c 452. d 453. b 454. a 455. d 456. a 457. b 458. c
   459. a   460. c 461. a   462. c   463. d   464. b   465. a
   466. b   467. c   468. a   469. d   470. b

ANSWERS TO COMPLETION TEST (p. 151-152)

   471. Handel, public 472. opera 473. music 474. music
   475. chorus 476. eight 477. "prima donna" 478. orchestra
   479. singspiel 480. opera buffa

CHAPTER 17

INTRODUCTION TO NINETEENTH-CENTURY ROMANTICISM IN MUSIC

Summary

Chapter 17 begins with an overview of Romanticism, in all its variety and contraditions. Romantic attitudes toward art, the social and political forces that shaped these attitudes, such as, the rural and urban creations of the industrial revolution. Many artists derived inspiration from their own countries cultural heritages, other aspired to universal visions.

The characteristics of Romantic music are all explored at length. The exaltation of the individual is traced to the writings of Jean Jacques Rousseau and to the American and French revolutions. Other trends in Romantic art (the worship of nature, exoticism, the interest in the supernatural) are discussed, as is the conceit of the Romantic hero, exemplified in the character of Byron, as well as in his works. The rise of the middle class and the declines of the patronage system are related directly to the artist's new self-image, as explorer and social critic rather than entertainer. New developments in painting, as revealed in the works of Fuseli, Goya, and Delacroix, are cited, as are the literary contributions of Goethe, Baudelaire, and the English poets, Wordsworth, Coleridge, Byron, Keats, and Shelley.

The orchestra itself was becoming a virtuoso's instrument. The Romantic era saw the emergence of a new type of performing artist: the symphonic conductor. Mendelssohn and Berlioz were both pioneers of conducting. Liszt, Wagner, and Mahler continued the trend.

Choruses also grew greatly in number and size in the Romantic period. Choral societies with hundreds of members appeared in Europe and the United States: Boston's Handel and Haydn Society was founded as early as 1815.

Although military and town bands of wind and percussion instruments had existed in previous centuries, there was a major increase in the number of bands in the nineteenth century. This was due in part to improved technology in wind instruments. Of great importance was the fact that valves were added to brass instruments, allowing them to play chromatically and in every key.

Included is a comparison chart of Classical and Romantic music. New forms were program music, and symphonic poems. Choral music, such as the Mass, took on symphonic dimensions. Both the Mass and oratorio became somewhat more secular, longer, and more imaginative. Opera flourished as never before under the genius of such composers as Wagner, Verdi, and

Puccini.

New trends in nineteenth century American music were: founding of the Handel and Haydn Choral Societies of Boston in 1815, organization of the Chicago Symphony Orchestra by Theodore Thomas, black music of Stephen Foster, exotic Romantic piano style of Louis Gottschalk, the band music of John Philip Sousa, and the music of the prototypical American composers of the period, Edward MacDowell.

Goals and Suggestions for Classroom Experiences

1. A striking example of Romantic melody can be found in the opening movement of Dvořák's Czech Suite, Op. 39. A long, flowing, lyrical melody unwinds at the outset, is repeated, twice varied, and then repeated still another time. The second variation of the melody is longer and would seemingly unwind into infinity, were it not interrupted by the return of the original melody. Does this resemble any Classical melody the students have encountered?

2. A fine example of the short Romantic piano piece is Brahms' Intermezzo in B♭ Minor, Op. 117, No. 2. Can the students determine the means by which Brahms achieved such an extraordinary degree of unity in this work? One factor is the constant presence of the melodic half step and whole step, either ascending or descending, in the melody and accompaniment. The "second theme," in D♭ major, is built from an augmentation of this stepwise motion.

3. At the opposite end of the spectrum of size of performing group is Berlioz' Grand symphonie funèbre et triomphale, Op. 15, an excellent example of a Romantic work on a grandiose scale. The work was first performed out-of-doors, in a funeral procession commemorating the tenth anniversary of the July Revolution of 1830. The fact that it was composed for band explains the absence of strings in the instrumentation. The first movement should be sampled, noting especially the use of percussion. In the final "Apothéose" of the symphony, note the astonishing effect created by the massive forces of a huge wind band, an expanded percussion section, and a six-part chorus (divided sections of sopranos, tenors, and basses).

Discussion Questions

1. What are the general characteristics of the Romantic temperament? Are there "general characteristics" that typify the temperament of our own times? If so, how do they compare with those of the Romantic period?

2. Was there any truth in the claim of the Romantics that the Classical style was "artificial?" Was there nothing artificial in Romanticism?

3. Music is sometimes called "the most romantic of all the arts." In what sense is this true?

4. The history of music is seen by some as an alternation between classically oriented periods and more romantic periods. Was the Baroque period romantic? To what extent?

5. Romantic music today forms a large part of the standard concert repertoire. Why? At this stage in the course, do you prefer Romantic music to Classical music? to Baroque?

Listening Questions

1. Suggested Example: Beethoven, Symphony No. 5 in C Minor, Op. 67, third movement, opening

   Due in part to the halting manner in which it begins, this melody by Beethoven offers a good example of Romantic melody.
   *True   False

2. Suggested Example: Smetana, Má Vlast, "The Moldau," opening

   The style of this work is more Romantic than Classical.
   *True   False

3. Suggested Example: Dvořák, Czech Suite, Op. 39, first movement, opening

   The most strikingly Romantic feature of the beginning of this movement is the chromatic melody.
   True   *False

4. Suggested Example: Mozart, Exultate, Jubilate, K. 165, first movement, opening

   The style of this work is more Romantic than Classical.
   True   *False

5. Suggested Example: Mendelssohn, Elijah, Op. 70, opening

   The opening of this work by Mendelssohn reflects his interest in Baroque music.
   *True   False

ANSWERS TO OBJECTIVE TEST (p. 153-155)

481. c 482. b 483. a 484. b 485. d 486. a 487. c 488. b
489. c 490. a 491. a 492. d 493. b 494. c 495. d
496. b 497. c 498. a 499. d 500. b

ANSWERS TO COMPLETION TEST (p. 155   )

501. perceiving, dealing 502. Rousseau 503. middle class
504. authors, critics 505. exotic 506. Victor Hugo
507. folk melodies 508. simple, complex 509. virtuoso
510. Boston

CHAPTER 18

PIANO MUSIC: CHOPIN AND LISZT

Summary

Chapter 18 surveys the results of the nineteenth-century composer's preoccupation with short works for the piano. Beethoven's sonatas and shorter works are cited at the beginning as a bridge between Classical and Romantic styles. The main part of the chapter, however, is concerned with the life and music of Frédéric Chopin and Franz Liszt.

Liszt made notable contributions to Romantic orchestral literature and wrote several sacred and secular choral pieces (though these are rarely heard today). He excelled in large scale composition and, not surprisingly, ignored chamber music as a medium.

Chopin's Nocturne in E^b Major, Op. 9, No. 2 and Liszt's Hungarian Rhapsody No. 6 in D^b Major are singled out for special consideration.

Goals and Suggestions for Classroom Experiences

1. To show the range of feeling encompassed by Chopin's nocturnes, the Nocturne in E^b Major can be contrasted with the Nocturne in C Minor, Op. 48, No. 1. The march-like B section of the latter (marked Poco più lento) is especially noteworthy with its gradual buildup of tension and dynamics. You may want to point out the way in which this increased energy is transferred to the varied repetition of the A section by means of the agitato triplet accompaniment.

2. Chopin's Polonaise in F# Minor, Op. 44 presents a particularly valuable example for classroom use in that it furnishes examples of two characteristic Polish dances: the polonaise and the mazurka, the second of which forms the A-major middle section of the piece (marked Doppio movimento - Tempo di mazurka). The drumming, rhythmic accompaniment to the polonaise theme is the characteristic rhythm for this stately dance.

3. Schubert's Fantasia in C Minor, D. 760 (the "Wanderer") and Liszt's Sonata in B Minor are works that may be profitably compared and contrasted, since each is based on the virtuosic elaboration of a unifying theme. Liszt's technique of thematic transformation can be readily contrasted with Schubert's more traditional ornamental variation technique. Schubert's work is, of course, far from easy

to play, but the overwhelming virtuosity of Liszt's piano style should be apparent to the students.

4. Brahms' piano music has often been criticized for being "unpianistic." A characteristic example of his style is in <u>Rhapsody in G Minor</u>, Op. 79, No. 2, which, although it falls into the category of the short Romantic piano piece, is actually composed in sonata form. The key scheme and developmental techniques can be explored in the usual fashion, with attention given to the fact that Brahms even used the traditional repeat sign at the end of the exposition. What elements of the piece contribute to its rhapsodic character? How "pianistic" or "unpianistic" is the work?

Discussion Questions

1. Why do you think Beethoven's piano sonatas were occasionally given subtitles, such as "Tempest," "Appassionata," or "Moonlight?"

2. How similar were the careers and life-styles of Chopin and Liszt? In what ways did their performance and compositional styles differ?

3. What does it mean to say that Liszt wrote for the piano in an "orchestral manner?" Did Beethoven? Did Chopin?

4. The piano music of Chopin and Liszt, though difficult to play, is undeniably "pianistic." How would you define that term on the basis of what you have heard so far?

5. Has the music you have studied in this chapter given you any further insight into the distinctions that can be drawn between the concepts "Classical" and "Romantic?" Can you cite any specific examples of Classicism in some of the Romantic music you have heard?

Listening Questions

1. Suggested Example: Liszt, <u>Hungarian Rhapsody No. 6 in D^b Major</u>, opening

    The tempo of the opening section of Liszt's <u>Hungarian Rhapsody No. 6 in D^b Major</u> is
    a. very fast.   *c. moderate.
    b. fast.   d. very slow.

2. Suggested Example: Schumann, <u>Carnaval</u>, Op. 9, opening

    The texture of the beginning section is largely

a. contrapuntal.   *c. homophonic.
b. monophonic.   d. pointillistic.

3. Suggested Example: Liszt, <u>Hungarian Rhapsody No. 15 in A Minor</u>, opening

This work was probably written by
a. Chopin.   *b. Liszt.

4. Suggested Example: Chopin, <u>Polonaise in A Major</u>, Op. 40, No. 1 "Vivo"

The meter of this piece is
a. duple.   c. compound.
*b. triple.   d. changing.

5. Suggested Example: Chopin, <u>Prelude No. 1 in C Major</u>, Op. 28, No. 1

This work was probably written by
*a. Chopin.   b. Liszt.

ANSWERS TO OBJECTIVE TEST (p. 156-158)

511. a 512. d 513. b 514. d 515. a 516. d 517. c 518. a
519. b 520. a 521. c 522. d 523. b 524. c 525. a
526. c 527. a 528. d 529. c 530. b

ANSWERS TO COMPLETION TEST (p. 158   )

531. descriptive 532. shorter 533. legato 534. rubato
535. nocturnes 536. études 537. dance forms 538. larger
539. symphonies 540. rhapsody

CHAPTER 19

THE ART SONG: SCHUBERT AND SCHUMANN

Summary

     Although brief mention is made of the development of the
art song in France during the nineteenth and early twentieth
centuries, the emphasis in Chapter 19 is on the Lied as it
flourished during the German Romantic movement. This development is related to the exuberant outburst of German lyric
poetry by such writers as Goethe, Schiller, and Heine in the
early nineteenth century.
     Strophic song has already been discussed in a previous
chapter; here, the possibilities of modified strophic and
freely composed structures are discussed, as is the important
role of the piano accompaniment. The careers and songs of
Schubert and Schumann are surveyed, with special attention to
Schubert's Die schöne Müllerin cycle, particularly the first
song in the cycle, "Das Wandern," and to Schumann's "Widmung."
     Though his lyrical melodies and profound accompaniments
mark Schubert as a Romantic composer, he was far closer than
Chopin or Liszt to the Classical tradition. Alongside his
dances and other short piano pieces, he wrote piano sonatas
which are Classical in structure. Not surprisingly, he also
wrote much chamber music, including many string quartets, a
masterful string quintet, and a well known piano quintet
called Die Forelle ("The Trou," 1819) after his own song whose
theme is the basis for the variations of its fourth movement.
Nine symphonies, of which the last two are acknowledged
masterpieces, six masses, and even fragments of operas add to
the list. But his over 600 songs are Schubert's greatest
vocal achievement.
     The subsequent history of the German art song is traced
through the works of Brahms, Wagner, Wolf, Mahler, and
Strauss.

Goals and Suggestions for Classroom Experiences

1.   Schubert's "Die Forelle" ("The Trout") affords one of
     countless examples of the composer's pictorial treatment
     of a piano accompaniment. Without having heard the title
     or seen the text, can the students guess at the nature of
     the song's subject matter on the basis of the piano figur-
     ations? The accompaniment is undoubtedly meant to depict
     the fish darting through the clear water. Can the stu-
     dents determine from the musical setting the moment when
     the fish is caught by the angler? Comparison made with
     the theme and variations movement from Schubert's "Trout"

<u>Quintet</u>, D. 667 for piano and strings should help demonstrate the potential for variation treatment inherent in the original material. Note that it is only in the final variation that the original piano setting is used.

2. Another song that formed the basis for a movement of a Schubert chamber work is the "Der Tod und das Mädchen" ("Death and the Maiden"). The slow piano introduction is notable for its harmonic simplicity and persistent use of dactylic rhythm. The accompaniment then becomes animated to portray the maiden's agitation in confronting death and finally returns to the obsessive dactyls as death speaks. In this work, Schubert employed a device he also used in the "Erlkönig," namely the use of the major mode to portray the seductive intentions of death in the concluding measures of the song. Again, comparison can be made with the variations on the song found in the second movement of Schubert's <u>"Death and the Maiden" Quartet</u>, D. 810. Can the students tell which elements of the original song Schubert selected to form the basis of the variations?

3. Schumann's "Die beiden Grenadiere" ("The Two Grenadiers") represents the view of three persons: the narrator and the two French soldiers returning to their defeated homeland during the Napoleonic Wars. What pictorial possibilities does this scenario present to Schumann? Do the students recognize the <u>Marseillaise</u> when it appears at the climax of the song? Is the sixteenth-note figure in the accompaniment supposed to represent a drum roll? Comparison can be made with another martial song by Schumann, "Der Soldat" ("The Soldier"). Astra Desmond has observed that "the postlude suggests the sagging body of the victim" (<u>Schumann Songs</u>, Seattle: University of Washington Press, 1972, p. 36). Do the students agree?

4. Brahms' <u>Four Serious Songs</u>, Op. 121, published the year before he died, represent the composer at his mellowest. Here, the accompaniment is not blatantly pictorial but crucial in establishing the mood of each song. Note particularly the third song, "O Tod, wie bitter," evenly divided in its portrayal of the bitterness of death and the good it accomplishes. The first half is dominated by falling motives, and, not surprisingly, the second half by rising motives. The subtle beauty of the shift, however, is not at all hackneyed. Observe the manner in which the piano shifts the mood before the text announces the change. You may want to ask the students to consider the difficulties of dealing with a biblical text in the intimate medium of the Lied. In what ways has Brahms surmounted these difficulties?

5. Hugo Wolf's style is well represented in his "Jägerlied" ("Hunter's Song"), the fourth of the Mörike Lieder. Especially notable are the many subtle tempo changes in this short work. Can the students explain the device Wolf used to depict the soaring eagle (sequential transposition, up a major third)? Can they identify the means by which he obtained unity in the piece (repetition of the same rhythmic pattern within the asymmetric $\frac{5}{4}$ meter)? Wolf breaks the unifying metric pattern in the twelfth measure. What explanation can students offer for this depature?

Discussion Questions

1. In what sense did Schubert's career reflect the Romantic notion of the "artist as hero?" In what sense did Schumann's?

2. In Lied, the partnership between poetry and music is necessary just as for the first time, the piano part is as important as the vocal line, why?

3. Lied composers were attracted to the work of the best poets of their day, but they also frequently used material of mediocre quality. Must a great art song be based upon an equally great text? What makes a poem suitable for musical setting?

4. To what extent do song texts resemble opera librettos? How do they differ? Which is more crucial to the success of the work?

5. How do the song texts that you have seen reflect the Romantic spirit as you understand it?

Listening Questions

1. Suggested Example: Mahler, Symphony No. 1 in D Major, first movement, opening through first theme

   The composer of this symphony used as his first theme the melody from one of his songs. The composer is probably
   a. Schubert.   c. Liszt.
   b. Schumann.   *d. Mahler.

2. Suggested Example: Schumann, "Widmung," opening

   This song was composed by
   a. Schubert   *b. Schumann.

3. Suggested Example: Schubert, "Erlkönig," opening

The piano accompaniment of this song by Schubert might be taken to represent
*a. a horse's hoofbeats.
b. the babbling of a brook.
c. approaching footsteps.
d. the gently falling rain.

4. Suggested Example: Brahms, <u>Four Last Songs</u>, Op. 121, No. 1, "Den es gehet dem Menschen," opening

   This song by Brahms might have as its subject
   a. love.   *c. death.
   b. happiness.   d. homesickness.

5. Suggested Example: Schubert, <u>Die Winterreise</u>, No. 2, "Die Wetterfahne," opening

   This song was composed by
   *a. Schubert.   b. Schumann.

ANSWERS TO OBJECTIVE TEST (p. 159-160)

541. c 542. a 543. c 544. d 545. b 546. a 547. d 548. c
549. b 550. d   551. a   552. d   553. b   554. c   555. b
556. d 557. c   558. a   559. b   560. a

ANSWERS TO COMPLETION TEST (p. 161   )

561. chanson 562. poetic, music 563. Schubert 564. piano
565. freely structured 566. piano, voice 567. pictorial
568. autobiographical 569. dichterliebe   570. Brahms

CHAPTER 20

SYMPHONY AND CONCERTO: BRAHMS AND TCHAIKOVSKY

Summary

Chapter 20 opens with a discussion of the origins of the Romantic symphony, as found in the symphonies of Beethoven and Schubert. The program symphony is mentioned, but since program music will be taken up in the next chapter, the concern here is essentially with the abstract symphony. Its development in the nineteenth century is traced through the more traditional symphonies of such composers as Mendelssohn and Schumann to the late nineteenth-century symphonies of Franck, Bruckner, Mahler and Dvorak. The characteristics of both the Romantic symphony and the Romantic concerto are described, and there are detailed discussions of three works: Brahms' Symphony No. 3 in F Major, Op. 90, Tchaikovsky's Symphony No. 6 in B Minor, Op. 74, (the "Pathetique"), and Tchaikovsky's Violin Concerto in D Major, Op. 35.

Goals and Suggestions for Classroom Experiences

1. The following diagram of the first movement of Brahms' Symphony No. 3 in F Major can be used to show important harmonic departures from the Classical use of sonata form. As in earlier diagrams, key shifts are represented by changes in the height of the lines; areas of modulation and uncertain key are represented by broken lines. As the students can see, contrary to traditional practice, Brahms modulates first, not to the dominant, but to the third degree, the mediant major. Another shift to the mediant minor in the closing section brings him a little closer to his original key, F major. The Romantic fondness for relationships in thirds is even more evident in the recapitulation, where, for the reprise of his second theme, Brahms actually modulated away from the tonic to D major, the submediant major, another shift of a third. A brief modulation back to the tonic at the end of the second theme and beginning of the closing section is not shown in this simplified diagram.

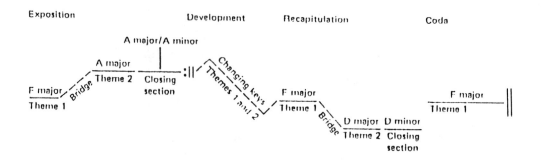

Exposition   Development   Recapitulation   Coda

2. A sampling of Schubert's symphonies can help pinpoint his role as a transitional composer. His Symphony No. 5 in B♭ Major, D. 485 is sufficiently small-scaled to be analyzed in some detail. Do the students find any evidence of the Romantic spirit in this work? They should have little difficulty finding such evidence in Schubert's later symphonies. The last two can be sampled almost at random to discover Romantic traits.

3. The students should recognize some old material in a new guise in Mendelssohn's Symphony No. 5 in D Minor, Op. 107 (the "Reformation"). The symphony makes use of the chorale tune "Ein' feste Burg," which the students have already encountered in Bach's Cantata No. 80 in Chapter 9. Despite its number, this was Mendelssohn's second symphony, and does not represent his mature style. How do the students react to the symphony? Do all the devices hold together, or is the work merely a pastiche? Was Mendelssohn's reverence for the Baroque misplaced here? Many critics have argued that it was.

4. Brahms' Piano Concerto No. 2 in B♭ Major, Op. 83 has four movements, the extra movement being a Scherzo following the first movement. For this reason, and because the solo part is so completely integreated into the orchestra, the work is generally regarded as a "symphony" for piano and orchestra. In the slow movement, you may want to point out the cello solo that, in effect, transforms this section into a sort of double concerto. Why did Brahms use the solo cello, rather than the cello section? Is the work a concerto or a symphony? How idiomatic is Brahms' piano writing? Would a piano soloist necessarily enjoy playing this work?

5. If Brahms' true medium was the orchestra, Chopin's was certainly the piano. Either of Chopin's piano concertos can be contrasted to Brahms'. Where Brahms obtained balance, perhaps to the pianist's chagrin, Chopin wrote

brilliant piano music and an indifferent orchestral accompaniment. How do the students react to the comparison?

Discussion Questions

1. Why do you suppose Schubert's symphonies were not appreciated in his own time?

2. Brahms has been described as the arch-conservative of the Romantic movement and, facetiously, as a composer whose only contribution to the history of music was a series of masterworks. How important is it for a composer to be an explorer, a breaker of new ground? What parallels can you draw between the careers and historical positions of Bach and Brahms?

3. How programmatic can a symphony be without a program? What programmatic aspects does Tchaikovsky's "Pathétique" Symphony contain aside from its subtitle?

4. Why did the Romantic composers of symphonies write so few works, compared to the early Classical composers of symphonies?

5. Which do you think is more difficult to obtain: an "ideal" performance of a Mozart violin concerto or an "ideal" performance of a Tchaikovsky violin concerto? Why?

Listening Questions

1. Suggested Example: Tchaikovsky, "Pathétique" Symphony, second movement, opening

   The most unusual feature of this movement by Tchaikovsky is its
   a. melody   c. harmony.
   *b. meter.   d. orchestration.

2. Suggested Example: Brahms, Symphony No. 3 in F Major, third movement, opening

   This movement from Brahms' Third Symphony is the
   a. first   *c. third.
   b. second.   d. fourth.

3. Suggested Example: Tchaikosvky, "Pathétique" Symphony, last movement, opening

   This movement from Tchaikovsky's "Pathétique" Symphony is the
   a. first.   c. third.

b. second.   *d. fourth.

4. Suggested Example: Tchaikovsky, <u>Violin Concerto in D
    Major</u>, third movement, opening

    The meter of this movement is
    *a. duple.   c. compound.
    b. triple.   d. irregular.

5. Suggested Example: Brahms, <u>Concerto in A Minor for Violin
    and Cello</u>, Op. 102 (the "Double"), first movement, opening

    This is a movement from a concerto by
    a. Chopin.   *c. Brahms.
    b. Schumann.   d. Tchaikovsky.

ANSWERS TO OBJECTIVE TEST (p.162-164)

   571. c 572. b 573. a 574. d 575. a 576. b 577. d 578. a
   579. c 580. b 581. d 582. c 583. a 584. c 585. b
   586. d 587. a 588. b 589. c 590. d

ANSWERS TO COMPLETION TEST (p. 164)

   591. Schubert 592. two 593. dense 594. repetition,
   variation 595. A German Requiem 596. Tchaikovsky
   597. Shakespeare 598. melody 599. double stopping
   600. orchestral music

PROGRAM MUSIC: MENDELSSOHN, BERLIOZ, AND SAINT-SAËNS

Summary

In chapter 21, the rising interest in program music exhibited by Romantic composers is ascribed, in part, to their
preoccupation with the literature of their time and, indeed,
their interest in the arts. Program music is defined as
music that is purely instrumental, yet closely associated
with nonmusical ideas. The development of program music is
traced from Beethoven's "Pastoral" Symphony to the tone poems
of Richard Strauss. The various types of program music are
discussed, and several examples are analyzed in detail: the
concert overture and incidental music as seen in the Overture,
"Scherzo," "Nocturne," and "Wedding March" from Mendelssohn's
A Midsummer Night's Dream, the program symphony as seen in
Berlioz' Symphonie fantastique, Op. 14, the symphonic poem as
seen in Saint-Saëns' Danse macabre, Op. 40. Liszt's Les
Preludes is also discussed in the section on the symphonic
poem, though in less detail.

Goals and Suggestions for Classroom Experiences

1. Beethoven's Coriolan Overture, Op. 62 was based on a play
   by von Collin. If that play is inaccessible, a synopsis
   of Shakespeare's tragedy of the same name can serve to
   highlight the main events of the drama. Can the students
   identify the specific developments in the plot that
   Beethoven used in his music? For Richard Wagner, the
   music depicted the climactic meeting of Coriolanus and
   his wife before the gates of his city. Does this seem
   plausible to the students?

2. The subtitle of the introduction to the first part of
   Berlioz' "dramatic symphony" Roméo et Juliette bears the
   following inscription: "Combats - Tumulte - Intervention
   du Prince." Note the appropriateness of the opening
   Allegro fugato as "music to duel by." Can the class
   identify the entry of the prince?

3. The fourth movement of Berlioz' Roméo et Juliette, the
   "Queen Mab Scherzo," is deservedly famous for a number of
   reasons. Students should note especially the extreme
   delicacy of the orchestration. How does the technique
   used here compare with that used by Mendelssohn to
   achieve a similar delicacy in the "Scherzo" from A Mid-
   Summer Night's Dream?

4. Each of the three movements of Liszt's Faust Symphony was intended to represent the character of one of the main figures in the Faust legend. After a brief review of the plot of Goethe's Faust, can the students offer suggestions about the figure that may be protrayed in each of the movements?

5. Students may also enjoy hypothesizing about Strauss's Till Eulenspiegels lustige Streicher, Op. 28. Before reading the program notes, listen to the first several sections to observe the colorful orchestration and to speculate about what ideas the program might include. Then read the program and listen again to the work while associating Strauss's ideas with the music.

Discussion Questions

1. Of Liszt, Berlioz, and Saint-Saëns, which do you think was the most original? Which do you think had the strongest and most lasting impact on music that follows?

2. What elements of the Romantic spirit do you find in the program for the Symphonie fantastique?

3. How crucial is knowledge of the program to full enjoyment of programmatic music?

4. Program music is still being written, although not nearly as frequently as in the nineteenth century. What types of programs would contemporary composers be likely to choose as the basis for their music?

5. In general, do you prefer "absolute" or "programmatic" symphonic music? Why?

Listening Questions

1. Suggested Example: Berlioz, Symphonie fantastique, fourth movement, opening

   This movement represents a march.
   *True   False

2. Suggested Example: Berlioz, Symphonie fantastique, last movement, opening

   This work was composed by Franz Liszt.
   True   *False

3. Suggested Example: Strauss, Till Eulenspeigel, opening

In this passage from Strauss' Till Eulenspeigel, one hears much contrast between individual instruments, part of the orchestra, and the entire orchestra.
*True   False

4. Suggested Example: Mendelssohn, A Midsummer Night's Dream, "Scherzo," opening

   This is the overture to Mendelssohn's A Midsummer Night's Dream.
   True   *False

5. Suggested Example: Strauss, Don Juan, Op. 20, opening

   This work was composed by
   *a. Richard Strauss.   c. Camille Saint-Saëns
   b. Felix Mendelssohn.   d. Hector Berlioz.

ANSWERS TO OBJECTIVE TEST (p. 165-167)

601. b 602. a 603. c 604. d 605. a 606. d 607. a 608. b
609. d 610. c 611. d 612. a 613. c 614. b 615. c
616. a 617. d 618. b 619. d 620. c

ANSWERS TO COMPLETION TEST (p. 167   )

621. arts 622. verbal descriptions 623. program music
624. theater 625. incidental music 626. more, fewer
627. idée fixe 628. Les Troyens 629. one
630. Thus Spake Zarathustra

CHAPTER 22

OPERA AND CHORAL MUSIC OF THE NINETEENTH CENTURY

Summary

Chapter 22 covers an unusually large amount of material, in part, because students are already likely to have some knowledge of Romantic opera to build upon, and in part, because of the great number of worthy operas produced by different composers during the period. Five works are singled out for special attention: Bizet's Carmen, Verdi's La Traviata, Puccini's La Bohème, and two works by Wagner, Tristan und Isolde and Die Walküre

Following a brief discussion of the operas of the pre-Romantic composers, Mozart and Beethoven, the broad survey of nineteenth century opera turns first to French opera. Grand opera and opera comique are considered, along with the intermediate form, lyric opera. A detailed discussion of Bizet's Carmen is then undertaken. The treatment of Italian opera opens with a discussion of the various contributions of composers such as Rossini, Donizetti, Bellini. The focus, however, is on Verdi, whose opera La Traviata is discussed in detail. Puccini's La Bohème is also considered. The discussion of German opera is almost entirely devoted to Wagner's career and works.

Two features of German Romantic opera stand in sharp contrast to the Italian style as Verdi was refining it. Mood, atmosphere, setting, and symbolic content take precedence over characterization and human conflicts. Accordingly, vocal melody is of lesser importance in projecting the message of the work. The orchestra is no mere accompaniment, a continuous melody, a part of the fabric of the drama, and the significance of its music is thus increased. Of this Wagner's music-dramas are the ultimate example. Included are detailed analyses of the "Ride of the Valkyries" from Die Walküre and the Prelude to Tristan and Isolde.

The discussion of Romantic choral works is necessarily much shorter, giving particular attention to the large-scale sacred works of Berlioz, Bruckner, Fauré, Elgar, Mendelssohn, Brahms, and Verdi.

Goals and Suggestions for Classroom Experiences

1. The text mentions the powerful effect exerted upon the Romantic imagination by the supernatural effects in Mozart's Don Giovanni. The final scene of that opera, included in the listening suggestions in Chapter 16 of the manual, may well merit another hearing, this time with

particular attention to the forward-looking aspects of the work. How Romantic do the students find this ending? The concluding ensemble, as mentioned before, was probably an act of expediency on Mozart's part.

2. Berlioz' Les Troyens is available in an excellent recording (Philips 6709 002). Among the choice selections is the eleventh number of Act I, the "Finale." This is the famous "Trojan March," the crucial episode in the legend, in which the horse is dragged into the city of Troy. In his score, Berlioz specified the use of three subsidiary orchestras for this scene; note how effectively the movement of the procession is captured in the recording. Another possible selection is the sixteenth number of Act II, again the "Finale," in which Cassandra and the other Trojan women elect suicide in preference to capture by the invading Greek soldiers.

3. The "Finale" to the last act of Bellini's Norma provides an excellent contrast to the "Finale" of the second act of Les Troyens. Both scenes are concerned with voluntary ritual death: the Trojan women kill themselves by strangulation, by stabbing themselves, or by leaping from the parapet of their temple; Norman and Pollione elect death by fire. Despite the similarity in the plot lines of both scenes, note how Berlioz has integrated the orchestra, the women's chorus, and the invading Greek soldiers into one continuous symphonic development, while Bellini has relied upon the traditional set pieces of opera (recitative, aria, chorus), in which the voices predominate.

4. Wagner's vocal style, like the Berlioz selection just discussed, abandons set pieces and places the orchestra in a new role. The "Liebestod" from Wagner's Tristan und Isolde effectively illustrates this style. How do the students react to Wagner's revolutionary procedure? Having heard this, do they have a better understanding of the term "continuous melody"?

5. The opening movements of the Requiems by Berlioz, Verdi, and Fauré can be compared in an attempt to arrive at a recognition of the general stylistic characteristics of these three composers. Though Brahms' German Requiem is not a Mass, it may also merit consideration in this context.

Discussion Questions

1. How do the librettos used by Romantic composers compare with those used by Classical composers? How does the subject matter of Romantic opera resemble or differ from that

of Classical opera?

2. The dramatic conventions of opera were discussed in Chapter 16. Did these conventions become more difficult to accept in the Romantic era than in the Classical era, or less so?

3. Why were the Romantic composers so powerfully attracted to the works of Shakespeare? Was Shakespeare a "Romantic?"

4. Requiems make up a large part of the Romantic choral works that have come down to us. Why is the Requiem appropriate for Romantic treatment? Is it inherently dramatic?

5. After Wagner had done his work, were there any frontiers left for experimentation by future composers? If so, what were they?

Listening Questions

1. Suggested Example: Puccini, La Bohème, "Che gelida manina," opening

   This selection is sung by a bass.
   True   *False

2. Suggested Example: Verdi, La Traviata, "Ah, fors' è lui," opening

   This selection is sung by a mezzo-soprano.
   True   *False

3. Suggested Example: Mozart, Don Giovanni, "La ci darem la mano," opening

   This selection was written in the eighteenth century.
   *True   False

4. Suggested Example: Wagner, Die Meistersinger, Prelude to Act I, opening

   This selection is from an opera by Wagner.
   *True   False

5. Suggested Example: Verdi, Otello, Act IV, opening

   This selection from a Verdi opera is, like La Traviata, representative of the composer's middle period.
   True   *False

631. b 632. c 633. a 634. b 635. d 636. a 637. c 638. d
639. c 640. d 641. a 642. a 643. c 644. b 645. d
646. c 647. a 648. d 649. c 650. b

ANSWERS TO COMPLETION TEST (p. 170)

651. vocal 652. mood, setting 653. Grand opera
654. orchestra 655. folklike 656. Carl Maria von Weber
657. orchestra 658. twenty-two 659. Mass, oratorio
660. concert hall

CHAPTER 23

NATIONALISM AND LATE ROMANTICISM

Summary

Chapter 23 is divided into two sections, the first dealing with the nationalistic music of the Romantic period, the second with the contrasting musical styles of late Romanticism.

The first section begins by tracing Romantic nationalism to the national styles that developed in European music during the early Baroque period. The emergence of Germany as a dominant force in European musical life during the eighteenth century is noted, and a parallel is drawn between the political struggles of the nineteenth century and the burgeoning interest in folk music in nations and political regions throughout Europe. The characteristics of folk music are defined, and their adaptability to concert music explained. The contributions of the following composers are then covered: in Russia, Glinka and the Russian Five; in Bohemia, Smetana and Dvořák; in Spain, Albéniz and de Falla; in England, Elgar and Vaughan Williams; and in Scandinavia, the Norwegian Grieg and the Finnish Sibelius. Works given special attention in this part of the chapter are Mussorgsky's Pictures at an Exhibition, in the Ravel orchestration, and to a lesser amount, Sibelius's Finlandia.

In the second section of the chapter the extension and expansion of the German Late Romantic tradition by the composers Wagner, Bruckner, Strauss, and Mahler is stated. There is a brief discussion of Mahler's style and a more detailed discussion and analysis of his song cycles, especially his earlier cycle Lieder eines fahrenden Gesellen ("Songs of a Wayfarer").

The chapter closes with a brief discussion of Richard Strauss's operas and Arnold Schoenberg's new harmonic system - the twelve-tone serial technique. A brief mention is made of late Romantic composers in other countries: in Russia, Rachmaninoff, and Scribian; and MacDowell in America.

Goals and Suggestions for Classroom Experiences

1. The "Prologue" to Mussorgsky's Boris Godunov can be examined for its nationalistic aspects, as well as for what it reveals of Mussorgsky's vocal style. The modality of the theme that opens the opera and that of the theme in the first chordal entrance may be analyzed at length. The recitative-like character of these melodies, and of others appearing in the "Prologue," can be discussed in the light

of Mussorgsky's statement, as quoted in the text: "I explore human speech; thus I arrive at the melody created by this kind of speech, arrive at the embodiment of recitative in melody . . . . One might call this a melody justified by sense." Students should also note the presence of other folklike elements: bold dissonance, pentatonic scales, and pedal tones.

2. Another interesting example of music with "folk" elements is Dvořák's Quartet No. 6 in F Major, Op. 96 (the "American"). Dvořák lived for a time in New York City and in a Bohemian community in Iowa. Can the students identify, in the first movement, the elements of American Indian and black spiritual music? Do they find the use of this material compatible with the otherwise "Brahms-like" quality of the piece? Needless to say, Dvořák's Symphony No. 9 in E Minor, Op. 95 (the "New World") can be examined in like manner.

3. To some extent, Sibelius ties together the two halves of the chapter. Though he is discussed in the context of musical nationalism, his works also display many features of late - some would say belated - Romanticism. A sampling of his symphonies should make the point. His little-known Symphony No. 4 in A Minor, Op. 63 contains several experimental aspects. Note the chromaticism and lack of clear tonality in the opening section of the third movement. His last symphony, No. 7 in C Major, Op. 105, is also well worth studying, if only to explore its unusual one-movement form. It might well be asked why this was Sibelius's last symphony. The work appeared in 1924, and Sibelius lived until 1957. If he ever attempted an eighth symphony, no trace of it has appeared.

Discussion Questions

1. To what extent was Verdi a musical "nationalist?" What about Wagner?

2. Why did composers of this era turn to writing Nationalistic Music?

3. Not since Henry Purcell, in the late seventeenth century, had a native-born English composer achieved a major, international reputation than Edward Elgar. Why do you think so many years elapsed?

4. In the nineteenth century, many composers living on the fringe of the great German musical tradition turned to their native music in order to establish their own musical identities. To what sources, if any, can the

contemporary American composer turn?

5. Late Romanticism survived well into the twentieth century, and indeed is still alive today, in film scores, for example. What accounts for its staying power?

Listening Questions

1. Suggested Example: Elgar, <u>Pomp and Circumstance</u>, Op. 39, No. 1, opening

   This work was composed by a nationalistic composer from
   a. Russia   *c. England.
   b. Bohemia.   d. Scandinavia.

2. Suggested Example: Smetana, <u>The Moldau</u>

   The style of this work, from the 1870's, is closest to
   a. Russian nationalism   c. Romanticism
   *b. Bohemian nationalism   d. Late Romanticism

3. Suggested Example: Mussorgsky-Ravel, <u>Pictures at an Exhibition</u>, "Promenade," opening

   This work is best described as a(n)
   *a. programmatic work.   c. symphonic poem.
   b. abstract symphony.   d. concerto for orchestra.

4. Suggested Example: Mahler, <u>Symphony No. 9 in D Major</u>, third movement, opening

   This excerpt is probably taken from a work by
   a. Debussy   c. Brahms.
   b. Ravel.   *d. Mahler.

5. Suggested Example: Dvořák, <u>Slavonic Dance in C Major</u>, Op. 72, No. 7, opening

   This work is an example of the musical nationalism of
   a. England.   c. Finland.
   *b. Bohemia.   d. Spain.

ANSWERS TO OBJECTIVE TEST (p.171-172)

661. d 662. b 663. a 664. a 665. c 666. d 667. b 668. d
669. b 670. a 671. c 672. d 673. c 674. b 675. c
676. b 677. d 678. c 679. a 680. d

681. 1600 682. folk music 683. national dances 684. Russian
685. Mussorgsky 686. piano 687. Dvořák 688. Vaughan
  Williams 689. Grieg 690. chromaticism

CHAPTER 24

INTRODUCTION TO EARLY TWENTIETH-CENTURY MUSIC

Summary

Chapter 24 serves as a general introduction to the music of the early twentieth century. Attention is also given to related developments in the visual arts, architecture, litera-ture, and the dance, as well as to the political and social climate of the time. The principal stages in the growth of early twentieth century music are surveyed, and certain trends such as impressionism, emphasis on objectivity, primitivism, nationalism, futurism, gebrauchsmusik, or functional music, light and satirical style, music of a machine culture, jazz, neoclassicism, atonality, serialism, expressionism, electronic music, and music in our society.

The chapter continues with an analysis of various aspects of early twentieth-century melody, rhythm, harmony, texture, timbre, dynamics, and form.

Included is a comparison chart of Romantic music and early Twentieth-century music. Trends in twentieth-century American music are discussed with the French influence of Nadia Boulanger. Like the nationalistic composers in Europe, American composers such as George Gershwin based their work on native folk styles. Traditionalists such as Samuel Barber and Walter Piston adhered to music of the past. Roger Sessions, one of the leading Progressives developed styles more modern. A fourth general group, heading by Charles Ives, sought new experimental paths, and Henry Cowell's experiments on piano music were his most fruitful contributions to modern music.

The last part of the chapter investigates Impressionism through art and music. Music with its floating harmonic idiom, influence of nature, chord streams, increased disso-nance, changes in timbre, and freer forms. There is a detailed analysis of Debussy's _Prélude à l'apres-midi d'un faune_; "Feux d'artifice," from _Preludes_, Book II; a discussion of Les Six ("The Six"); and a brief discussion of Maurice Ravel, and his _Concerto in G_.

Goals and Suggestions for Classroom Experiences

1. Just as we observed the transition from Classical to Romantic in the works of Beethoven, we can observe the transition from late Romantic to early twentieth-century styles in the works of a number of individual composers. In the case of Schoenberg, the transition can be pointed out through a comparison of the early _Verklärte Nacht_, Op. 4 (1899) and the twelve-tone _Variations for Orchestra_, Op.

31 (1928). In the case of Stravinsky, the Symphony in E^b, Op. 1 (1907) can be contrasted with The Rite of Spring (1913). Since the concluding portion of The Rite is analyzed in detail in the text, the "Dance of the Adolescents" from the first part of the score might serve best here. Note the "primitivism" of the hammering rhythm heard at the opening of the dance. Also worthy of note are the use of ostinatos throughout the piece and the narrow range of its diatonic melodies.

2. As mentioned in Chapter 16, Beethoven was probably farthest ahead of his time in his late string quartets. A review of part of one of those works can offer an interesting approach to the quartets of Bartók. Bartók truly carried that standard medium into uncharted realms. An excellent example is the fourth movement, Allegro pizzicato, of his String Quartet No. 4. What similarities do the students find in the Beethoven and Bartók quartets? What differences do they find? In the light of Bartók's works, how "modern" were Beethoven's late quartets?

3. Honegger's Pacific 231 (Mouvement symphonique No. 1) can be used to illustrate the artistic interest in the "machine culture." Without having heard the title, can the students derive any specific associations from the work? Once they have heard the title, can they identify the musical means by which Honegger was able to suggest the motion of a great locomotive? Is this program music?

4. The influence of jazz on the composers of concert music can be illustrated through the use of Stravinsky's Ragtime for 11 Instruments, either in its original form or in the piano arrangement made by the composer in 1919. Also useful for this purpose are the ragtime dance from Stravinsky's L'Histoire du soldat, his Piano Rag, and Milhaud's La Creation du monde. Can the students define the jazz elements as the occur in these pieces?

5. The second of Debussy's orchestral Nocturnes, "Fêtes," offers a wealth of interesting details. Perhaps most interesting is the pairing of English horn with clarinet, and flute with oboe, combinations that lead in each case to the creation of an entirely "new," composite sound. The passage written in a meter of $\frac{15}{8}$ is also worth noting, as are the instrumentation at the beginning of the processional, and its subsequent buildup, the combination of the opening material of the piece with the processional theme, and the use of muted horns as the music fades away. What relationship do students find between this work and the Romantic nocturnes discussed in Chapter 19? The work can also be contrasted with a portion of Debussy's last

orchestral work, the "poème dansé" Jeux. How does the orchestral style of the mature Debussy compare with that displayed in the early nocturne?

Discussion Questions

1. What were the most important effects of the scientific achievements and political turmoil of the early twentieth century on art and music?

2. How do the aims and principles of "The Six" in early twentieth century France compare with those of "The Five" in nineteenth century Russia?

3. Many early twentieth century composers criticized late Romantic music as being overblown and pompous. Does the criticism have validity?

4. To what extent was musical Impressionism merely another manifestation of musical nationalism?

5. What factors help explain the great interest shown in rhythm and percussive sounds in the early twentieth century?

Listening Questions

1. Suggested Example: Schoenberg, Gurrelieder, Part III, "The Wild Chase," opening

   The style of this composition is best described as
   *a. late Romantic.   c. serial.
   b. Impressionist.   d. Futurist.

2. Suggested Example: Prokofiev, Classical Symphony, first movement, opening

   The type of this work is best described as
   a. late Romantic.   *c. Neoclassical.
   b. Impressionist.   d. Nationalistic.

3. Suggested Example: Honegger, Pacific 231 (Mouvement symphonique No. 1), opening

   This work is an example of the influence exerted upon music by
   a. nature   c. war.
   b. electricity.   *d. the machine.

4. Suggested Example: Stravinsky, Circus Polka, opening

This piece is <u>not</u> characterized by
*a. atonality.   c. shifting meters.
 b. dissonant harmonies.   d. uneven phrases.

5. Suggested Example: Orff, <u>Catulli Carmina</u>, Actus III,
    opening

    This piece is best characterized by the term
    a. Futurism.   c. Neoclassicism.
    b. aleatoric.   *d. primitivism.

<u>ANSWERS TO OBJECTIVE TEST</u> (p. 174-176)

    691. c 692. c 693. a 694. a 695. b 696. d 697. c 698. b
    699. c   700. a   701. b   702. c   703. a   704. b   705. b
     706. d   707. d   708. a   709. c   710. b

<u>ANSWERS TO COMPLETION TEST</u> (p. 176   )

    711. twentieth 712. Impressionist 713. American jazz
    714. atonal, serial 715. percussive 716. Barber 717. Piston
    718. harmonic 719. increased   720. freer

NEW STYLES OF TONALITY

Summary

Chapter 25 focuses on one of those two major groups of
early twentieth-century composers who "felt that their music
had to be based on some concept of tonality." (Coverage of
the other group, those concerned with atonality and serialism,
will be found in Chapter 26.) In chapter 25, the careers and
style traits of three major composers - Bartók, Hindemith, and
Stravinsky - are discussed at some length.
    Bartók, who was influenced by the nationalist movement in
his native Hungary was not limited to just Hungarian melodies
but also to a wide range of European and New Eastern styles.
In effect, Bartók achieved a synthesis of a variety of folk
styles and older and newer elements of the Western art music
tradition.
    Other devices that were used included: octave displace-
ment, polyrhythms, tone clusters, and a style of form. Other
works by Bartók were discussed briefly.
    The music of Stravinsky is wide and varied with an early
use of folk music. His early works were associated with dance
and ballet.
    The German composer, Paul Hindemith, was one of the
leaders of the twentieth-century, who attempted to make serious music more accessible to the general public with his
Gebrauchsmusik, or "music for use." He objected to the
strenuous use of Harmonic Innovation.
    Works chosen for analysis are Bartók's Music for Strings,
Percussion and Celesta, Hindemith's Mathis der Maler Symphony,
and Stravinsky's The Rite of Spring. The chapter concludes
with a discussion of other early twentieth-century composers
working within a tonal framework, with emphasis given to the
works of Ravel and Prokovief, Ives, Copland, Shostakovich,
and Britten.
    The musical style of Ives is discussed with an analysis
of his "Fourth of July" from A Symphony: Holidays.
    The works of Aaron Copland illustrate many of the trends
apparent in American music during the twentieth-century. His
melodies are both distinctive and attractive, his rhythms are
vital, and his harmonies are basically tonal. An analysis
of "Hoe Down" from Rodeo is discussed.
    Prokofiev's "Classical Symphony" is discussed.

Goals and Suggestions for Classroom Experiences

1. Perhaps the best introduction to Bartók's style is to be

found in his piano music. Several of the pieces in the sixth volume of his _Mikrokosmos_ can be analyzed to demonstrate the artistic results the composer was able to achieve with severely restricted means. For example, No. 141 is based entirely on the device of mirror writing, No. 143 on divided arpeggios, and No. 144 on minor seconds and major sevenths. Nos. 145a and 145b (which can be played either separately or together, on two pianos) demonstrate the possibilities of Bach's invention technique applied to a modern, chromatically inflected melodic style. No. 146 is based entirely on ostinati, while the last six pieces in the volume are dances "in Bulgarian rhythm" with the asymmetric combinations of beats in the various dances indicated in the time signatures.

2. Bartók's late _Sonata for Solo Violin_ may be regarded as Neoclassical, or better yet, as "Neo-Baroque," since it appears to be based on the tradition established by Bach in his works for solo violin. The second movement, an awsomely difficult fugue, is especially interesting. The work can be used to illustrate several elements of the composer's melodic and harmonic style, as well as the extreme demands he made upon the violinist. (The work was written for Yehudi Menuhin.)

3. Hindemith's style, like Bartók's, may be conveniently approached through his piano music. His _Sonata No. 3_, written in 1936, is quite characteristic of the composer's fully developed style. The first movement is a flexible adaptation of the sonata form, with a siciliano first theme serving as counterpoint to the second theme. The themes are recapitulated in reverse order, and the coda is based on the transition section, with a final reference to the siciliano theme at the end. The third movement is long and complicated in form, containing a marchlike first theme and a transition section in the form of a fugato, which anticipates material used in the fugal finale of the sonata. The finale is a long, sonorous double fugue, the second fugue being based on the fugato in the third movement.

4. The following diagram, a very general outline of the "Danse sacrale" from Stravinsky's _The Rite of Spring_, can be used to give students a somewhat clearer understanding of Stravinsky's use of form in this work. The form is basically determined by recurrence of material from the main A section. At its first repetition, the A section appears virtually intact, but its tonal center has been shifted down a half step, from D to C#. The A-section material next makes a very fragmentary appearance, once again centered upon D; this third appearance seems

something of a "false entry," since the C section picks up just where it had been before the seven-measure interruption. Finally, the A material appears in an extended form, this time centered upon the note A, the whole section serving as a sort of "dominant" preparation for the work's final chord, based upon the note D. The exact proportions of the various sections are difficult to establish due to the constantly shifting meters.

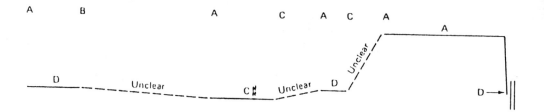

5. One of Stravinsky's Neoclassical works, the 1945 Symphony in Three Movements, can also be explored in a systematic way, charting the additive form of the first movement and noting especially its scheme of repetition. The second movement is in a simple ABA form, in chamber style. The A theme is characterized by the simultaneous use of D major and D minor, while the B section exploits the sonorities of the harp and other solo instruments. The third movement, which opens with a bimodal theme, can be studied with a special eye toward texture. Is the movement predominantly homophonic or polyphonic? How "Classical" do the students find this work? Many critics feel that the work harks back to the musical language of The Rite of Spring. Can students describe any aspects of this retrogressive tendency in the piece?

Discussion Questions

1. To what extent was Bartok's music a bridge between old and new styles of composition? between East and West?

2. What problems can arise when a composer is subjected to official scrutiny, as in the cases of Hindemith, Prokofiev, and Shostakovich? Is such scrutiny ever justifiable?

3. Why should Stravinsky have turned to serialism at the end

of his life? Was this turnabout surprising in light of
his earlier opposition to serialism? Was it predictable
in view of his constantly changing style?

4. Ravel's music is sometimes criticized as being all color
and no substance. Is there any validity to this
criticism?

5. Whic of the composers discussed in this chapter do you
consider the most revolutionary? Which do you consider
the most conservative?

Listening Questions

1. Suggested Example: Hindemith, Mathis der Maler Symphony,
first movement, opening

This movement from Hindemith's Mathis der Maler Symphony
features a borrowed melody.
*True   False

2. Suggested Example: Ravel, Piano Concerto in G, third
movement, opening

This work is written in a tonal style.
*True   False

3. Suggested Example: Bartók, Concerto for Orchestra, first
movement, opening

This selection is a good example of musical Primitivism.
True   *False

4. Suggested Example: Shostakovich, Symphony No. 9, Op. 70,
first movement, opening

This movement from a symphony by Shostakovich is Neoclassical in style.
*True   False

5. Suggested Example: Stravinsky, The Firebird, opening

This work is a good example of Futurism in music.
True   *False

ANSWERS TO OBJECTIVE TEST (p. 177-179)

721. b 722. c 723. d 724. a 725. d 726. b 727. c 728. a
729. b 730. c 731. a 732. d 733. b 734. b 735. c
736. a 737. b 738. c 739. a 740. b

ANSWERS TO COMPLETION TEST (p. 179)

741. Bartók 742. simple 743. polyrhythms 744. style, style
745. ballets 746. Hindemith 747. Charles Ives 748. jazzlike
749. American 750. Classical Symphony

CHAPTER 26

ATONALITY AND SERIALISM

Summary

Chapter 26 focuses on the music of composers who wrote
in an atonal style. The influence of Brahms and Wagner on the
young Schoenberg is described, and the gradual evolution of
Schoenberg's style is traced from Wagnerian, Romanticism,
through atonality, to his fully developed serial style.
Schoenberg's tie to the Expressionist school of painting is
cited as a contributing factor in this evolution. Sprechstimme, Klangfarbenmelodie, and the workings of the twelve-
tone system are explained, and Schoenberg's works and those of
his two disciples, Berg and Webern, are surveyed. Works
treated in detail are Schoenberg's Pierrot lunaire, Op. 21 and
Suite for Piano, Op. 25, Berg's Lyric Suite for String Quartet,
and Webern's Symphony, Op. 21. An evolution of the Symphony
chant is included.

The music of Schoenberg, Berg, and Webern, represents one
of the most significant, innovative trends in music in the
first half of the twentieth century. Their work has had and
continues to have far-reaching influence on the techniques and
methods of many subsequent composers.

Goals and Suggestions for Classroom Experiences

1. Schoenberg's Verklärte Nacht was recommended in Chapter
    25 of the manual as an example of the composer's late
    Romantic style. The work can be profitably taken up again
    at this point and contrasted with Schoenberg's later,
    atonal work. Equally fascinating in this context is his
    Chamber Symphony No. 2, Op. 38. The work was begun in
    1906, but left substantially unfinished. Schoenberg did
    not complete the work until 1935, well after he had formu-
    lated his twelve-tone system. The piece has two move-
    ments, both of which employ a developmental variation
    technique. Can the students find stylistic traces of
    Brahms, Strauss, and Wagner in the work? Still more in-
    teresting, can traces of Schoenberg's own serial style be
    found? Clearly, Schoenberg had not entirely lost his
    taste for late Romanticism by 1935. How do the students
    react to this work in comparison with his serial composi-
    tions?

2. The music of Schoenberg and his disciples is still far
    from being universally accepted by the general public, and
    the reason probably has something to do with the stressful

emotion it so often evokes. If students are still resist-
ing twelve-tone serial style after having heard a few
works, you might have them try Schoenberg's Survivor from
Warsaw, Op. 46, a work based on a tone row, with a narration written by Schoenberg himself. Recordings of the
work are available in English, and the narration, with its
supporting music, should speak for itself with little explanation. Do the students find the style appropriate to
this kind of work?

3. Berg's opera Wozzeck, shows many aspects of his style very
clearly. His lyricism is well represented in the third
scene of the first act. How far removed is this scene
from late Romanticism? Examples of the serial style can
be found in parts of Wozzeck. The fact that tonal music
is prominent in some scenes can give students an opportunity to try to distinguish between tonal and atonal passages.

4. Each of Webern's Five Pieces for Orchestra, Op. 10, is
very short, and every page of the score can be studied
with great profit. The following features of the music
are among the most noteworthy: the unusual orchestra,
including a large percussion section and solo strings in
place of the usual orchestral string section; the persistent use of flutter-tonguing in the winds, and harmonics
and other special effects in the strings; the extreme care
with which dynamics and subtle changes of tempo are indicated; the wide skips in the melodic lines and the pointillistic phrase structure; and finally the use of the
large percussion section to produce delicate effects.

5. Stravinsky's belated conversion to the twelve-tone serial
technique was mentioned in the previous chapter and will
be treated again in Chapter 30. One of his works that
incorporates aspects of the serial technique is the 1954
In Memoriam Dylan Thomas. Is his adoption of the technique totally convincing? Which of the many Stravinskys
do the students like best? In Memoriam can be readily
compared, in its lyricism and in its setting of the text,
to Berg's style in Wozzeck.

Discussion Questions

1. Schoenberg, Berg, and Webern made up the so-called "Second
Viennese School" of composition. Who made up the "First
Viennese School?" How did the "schools" differ?

2. Do you find any elements of Romanticism in the music of
the Second Viennese School? If so, what are they?

3. To a large extent, the "rules" of serial composition were drawn up <u>before</u> serial compositions themselves appeared. Did the rules of traditional harmony precede composition, or did they grow out of compositional practice?

4. Is the tone row of a serial composition intended to be heard as such? If not, how does it serve as an organizing principle? Does it function on a subconscious level?

5. Based upon your experience with twentieth-century music thus far, which of the following composers do you feel will have the greatest permanent impact on the course of musical history: Bartók, Hindemith, Stravinsky, Schoenberg, Berg, or Webern? Which will have the least? Why?

Listening Questions

1. Suggested Example: Schoenberg, <u>Chamber Symphony No. 2</u>, Op. 38, first movement, opening

   This selection is most representative of Schoenberg's preserial, atonal style of composition.
   True   *False

2. Suggested Example: Schoenberg, <u>Suite for Piano</u>, Op. 25, first movement, opening

   This excerpt is a good example of atonal style.
   *True   False

3. Suggested Example: Schoenberg, <u>Pierrot lunaire</u>, "Mondestrunken," opening

   The vocal technique in this excerpt can best be described as coloratura.
   True   *False

4. Suggested Example: Webern, <u>Symphony</u>, Op. 21, first movement, opening

   This composition is for string quartet.
   True   *False

5. Suggested Example: Berg, <u>Lyric Suite</u>, first movement, opening

   This selection offers a representative example of pointillistic texture.
   True   *False

ANSWERS TO OBJECTIVE TEST (p. 180-182)

751. a 752. c 753. d 754. b 755. c 756. d 757. a 758. b
759. c 760. a 761. b 762. d 763. c 764. b 765. d
766. a 767. c 768. a 769. b 770. c

ANSWERS TO COMPLETION TEST (p. 182)

771. Brahms, Wagner 772. happy 773. without tonality
774. soprano 775. retrograde 776. musical 777. classical
778. sparse 779. strict 780. stimulus

CHAPTER 27

MUSIC IN THE LATER TWENTIETH CENTURY

Summary

Chapter 27 surveys the output of the post-World War II musical avant-garde, from the works of students of Messaien to some of the latest works of Boulez, Stockhausen and Carter. The theories and experiments of Messiaen are analyzed, and the concept of "total serialization" is explained in connection with the music of Boulez and Stockhausen. Stravinsky's serial music, briefly mentioned in Chapter 25, is then taken up in some detail, with particular attention to his <u>Movements for Piano and Orchestra</u> (1959), which Stravinsky himself called his "most advanced work."
    Electronic music is then discussed, and a rationale offered for the production of music by electronic means. The various ways of producing electronic music are described, from Ussachevsky's musique concrète to the more recent music created by synthesizers. The latest developments in tape production and the use of computer programming to realize electronic works are also noted. Mario Davidovsky's <u>Synchronisms No. 1</u> for flute and tape is analyzed in detail. Developments in the production of electronically created sound have spurred composers to discover new ways of writing for conventional instruments. The text explores an example of the new instrumental music, Penderecki's experimental <u>Polymorphia</u> for strings. Contemporary experimentation in the use of other instruments is also noted, and experimental writing for the voice is observed in the works of Berio and Crumb. A collection of works similar in spirit to Berio's is the four books of <u>Madrigals</u> by Crumb. The madrigals are written for soprano solo, accompanied in each book by a different small ensemble. A detailed analysis of <u>Madrigals</u>, Book IV, by Crumb follows.
    Under the heading "New Principles of Structure," the controversial theories and music of John Cage are discussed, with particular attention to his use of indeterminacy. Also featured in this section is the music of Elliot Carter, whose <u>Double Concerto for Piano and Harpsichord</u> is analyzed in terms of Carter's concern with the problems of rhythmic and textural continuity.
    "Minimal" or "Systematic" music of Glass is discussed with an analysis of his <u>Modern Love Waltz</u> for flute, clarinet, violin, cello, and electric piano.
    The chapter concludes with a discussion of present trends and future possibilities.

Goals and Suggestions for Classroom Experiences

1. Difficulty in recommending avant-garde selections stems from the fact that recordings enter and leave the catalog with quicksilver rapidity. Boulez' <u>Structures</u>, for example, is not currently available. <u>Works by Boulez</u> can be discussed from the point of view of organization. Boulez' music is among the most thoroughly "organized" in the history of music. Does it sound it? In the liner notes to his recording of the <u>Sonata No. 1</u> (Columbia M-32161), Charles Rosen wrote of the "considerable freedom that the execution of Boulez' music requires." How does the freedom manifest itself?

2. The following very general schematic representation of Davidovsky's "Synchronisms No. 1" can be used in an extended analysis of the work. The lines represent the presence of tape or flute, or both, at any given time; important dynamic shifts are also given. The first section is the most varied dynamically. Despite the seemingly equal appearance of flute and tape in this section, the tape is the dominant factor in controlling both pace and dynamics. The texture is most evenly balanced in the B section, where both "instruments" contribute about equally, maintaining a rather loud dynamic level throughout. The flute dominates the final section, with the tape entering only at the end of the work as a kind of punctuation. Shifting textures and dynamics are only part of the entire work, of course, but representation of pitch and pitch center would be very difficulty in this work. Can students explain why?

A	B	C

Tape:
Flute:
Dynamics: p < fp < fp < fp < f < ff   p < fp < f   > p   p < f > p   f < ff p   < f p

3. One of the most remarkable compositions to surface in recent years is Berio's <u>Sinfonia</u>, a work recorded under the composer's direction by the New York Philharmonic and the Swingle Singers on Columbia MS-7268. <u>Sinfonia</u>, which has an extensive part for prerecorded tape, is in four movements. The first employs fragments from the written

works of the French anthropologist Claude Lévi-Strauss;
the second is intended as a memorial to Martin Luther
King, with the vocal part derived from manipulation of
his name; the fourth, a "sort of coda," has a text based
on brief selections from the texts used in preceding
movements. The third movement of the work is, according
to notes provided by the composer on the record liner,
"the most experimental music I have written." Berio
based it on the third movement of Mahler's Symphony No.
2, the "Resurrection" Symphony. An interesting comparison
can thus be made between the late Romantic and the avant-
garde styles.

4. A very valuable three-record set, entitled "The Avant
    Garde String Quartet in the U.S.A." is available from Vox
    (SVBX 5306). The album, the third in a series devoted to
    the development of the American string quartet from colo-
    nial times to the present, contains music by Brown, Cage,
    and Crumb, among others. The set offer numerous possi-
    bilities for stylistic comparisons.

5. John Cage is responsible for a work entitled Imaginary
    Landscape No. 4 (1951), a piece written for twelve radios,
    and performed by two people, one of whom controls the
    volume knobs, and the other the station selectors. You
    may want to ask students who own transistor radios to
    bring them to the next class and improvise their own
    Landscape. A discussion of the validity of such a work
    can follow.

Discussion Questions

1. Even with total serialization, is it possible to
    "organize" a work completely if live performers are in-
    volved? In any case, is it desirable to do so?

2. It has been argued, facetiously, that Cage's 4'33" is his
    finest work, and perhaps the finest work of avant-garde
    composition. What do you make of that statement?

3. How much "chance" can be involved before music begins to
    turn into noise? Is noise desirable?

4. Do any rules of composition still exist today? If so,
    what are they?

5. You have recently been exposed to the work of several
    highly respected contemporary composers. Which one seems
    to you to have the strongest grip on the key to the
    future? Why?

Listening Questions

1. Suggested Example: Davidovsky, <u>Synchronisms for Cello</u>
   <u>and Electronic Sounds, No. 1</u>, opening

   This work was probably composed by
   a. Cage.   c. Boulez.
   *b. Davidovsky.   d. Penderecki.

2. Suggested Example: Subotnick, <u>The Wild Bull</u>, Part II,
   opening

   This work is played by
   *a. only an electronic synthesizer.
   b. synthesizer and brass instruments.
   c. synthesizer and percussion instruments.
   d. synthesizer, brass, and percussion instruments.

3. Suggested Example: Cage, <u>Concerto for Prepared Piano and</u>
   <u>Chamber Orchestra</u>, opening

   This work was probably composed by
   a. Boulez.   *c. Cage.
   b. Carter.   d. Berio.

4. Suggested Example: Xenakis, <u>Bohor I</u>, opening

   This work is best described as
   a. aleatoric.   c. electronically synthesized.
   b. total serialization.   *d. musique concrète.

5. Suggested Example: Berio, <u>Circles</u>, opening

   This work was probably composed by
   a. Stravinsky.   c. Schoenberg.
   *b. Berio.   d. Davidovsky.

ANSWERS TO OBJECTIVE TEST (p. 183-185)

781. c 782. b 783. a 784. d 785. b 786. a 787. c 788. b
789. d 790. a 791. c 792. d 793. a 794. c 795. d
796. b 797. a 798. d 799. d 800. b

ANSWERS TO COMPLETION TEST (p. 185   )

801. Messiaen 802. total serialization 803. oriental
804. late 805. traditional 806. computer 807. mute
808. violin 809. free   810. chance

CHAPTER 28

AMERICAN POPULAR MUSIC

Summary

    Chapter 28 presents a survey of popular music in America, focusing on folk music, jazz, musical comedy, country and western, and rock. In the initial section of the chapter, the sources of America's popular music are traced to the white immigrants and black slaves who brought their anonymous and orally transmitted songs with them. The stylistic characteristics of various kinds of folk music are described, as are the various works in which these characteristics are manifested.

    The nature and sources of jazz are then discussed, followed by a detailed analysis of the various stages through which jazz has passed in the twentieth century. Special attention is given to Armstrong's "West End Blues," Henderson's "King Porter Stomp," and Parker's "Ornithology."

    Musical comedy is briefly treated before a discussion of the development of country and western music: its origins in early folk ballads, its dispersal throughout the country by means of radio, and the variant strains in which it exists today.

    The chapter concludes with a survey of rock music and its offshoots. The youth culture and the place of music in it are described, and the styles of a number of early musicians - Fats Domino, Bill Haley, and Presley - are discussed. The treatment of rock in the 1960s focuses on two somewhat antithetical groups - the Beatles and the Rolling Stones. The concluding portion of the section deals with the numerous forms of rock music that have developed in the last decade.

Goals and Suggestions for Classroom Experiences

1. A comparative study of early Anglo-American and black folk music, with charts and form diagrams, may prove useful. In what ways are the styles similar? In what ways have they merged in the creation of modern popular music?

2. Recent years have seen a renewed interest in ragtime. You may want to project a selection chosen from one of Joplin's rags and expand upon the text's discussion of the ragtime style. Can the students then identify these elements upon listening to a recording of one of Joplin's rags? Similar treatment can be given to the very important blues form.

3. The simple schematic diagram of Armstrong's "West End

Blues" given below can be used in a discussion of jazz form. The light lines at the top represent the main melody, which appears, substantially intact, three times. The broken lines represent the free improvisation that is carried on throughout the work. The bold lines at the bottom represent the basically unchanging harmonic and rhythmic framework of the piece, repeated four times after the original appearance. The most obvious of the improvisational passages are found in the trumpet solo of the introduction and the trombone and piano "variations" of the A^1 and A^3 sections, played as they are without the basic melody. It should be noted, however, that some degree of improvisation affects all aspects of the work, including the melody and the rhythmic accompaniment. Do the students agree that the work is in a theme and variations form? What other form does the work resemble?

4. Any of a number of early and late jazz compositions can be treated in comparative fashion. Can the student indentify the elements that distinguish each style? What elements are found in both the early and late styles?

5. Early and late rock music can also be treated in comparative fashion. What aspects of early rock music have been carried over into present works? Which aspects have been dropped?

Discussion Questions

1. To what do you attribute the current interest in ragtime, and in the music of Scott Joplin in particular?

2. A number of critics of modern jazz have stated that the

100

music has become too cerebral, too far removed from earlier, more popular styles. To what extent do you agree with this criticism?

3. What elements in the musical comedies of Rodgers and Hammerstein have made them so universally popular? Would the music itself be as popular without the intriguing lyrics?

4. What factors account for the current popularity of country and western music? Do you think the music will still be as popular fifty years from now?

5. How does modern disco music compare with other styles of rock? Is rock music losing some of the creative vitality it had in earlier years?

Listening Questions

Because the choice of recordings is likely to vary greatly from one record library to another, no specific listening questions have been included in Chapter 28.

ANSWERS TO OBJECTIVE TEST (p. 186-187)

811. a 812. b 813. c 814. b 815. a 816. d 817. b 818. c
819. b 820. a 821. d 822. a 823. c 824. b 825. a
826. c 827. d 828. b 829. a 830. d

ANSWERS TO COMPLETION TEST (p. 187-188)

831. conjunct 832. English ballad 833. twelve 834. I, IV, V
835. Bessie Smith 836. black folk music 837. West Africa
838. New Orleans 839. Louis Armstrong 840. 1950s

CHAPTER 29

ASPECTS OF MUSIC IN SOME NON-WESTERN CULTURES

Summary

   Chapter 29 serves as an introduction to the music of five
non-European cultures - those of Africa, the American Indian,
India, and China. In treating each of these cultures, the
instruments, theoretical bases and stylistic traits of its
music are described, along with a consideration of how music
is incorporated into the life of the people.
   There is an analysis of a Work Song from Burundi and
another of Ibihubi both from Africa. There is also a listening analysis of a Chinese piece based on a pentatonic scale,
Wild Geese Landing on the Sand Beach.
   The instructor's principal task will be to clarify, by
reference to appropriate recorded examples, the technical
points raised in the text. A number of readily available
recordings from which to choose selections are listed at the
end of the chapter.

Goals and Suggestions for Classroom Experiences

1.   Students might benefit from the construction of a chart
     comparing the treatment of musical elements in the five
     different cultural groups discussed in Chapter 6. A sixth
     column might be added for the traditional music of the
     West (i.e., Classical and Romantic) or for current popular
     music.

2.   Photographs of the instruments used in other cultures,
     accompanied by aural examples where possible, can be used
     to further the comparison of Western and non-Western
     music. Students should be able to categorize the instru-
     ments as chordophones, aerophones, idiophones, and mem-
     branophones, and to decribe in some fashion the ways in
     which the timbres of foreign instruments differ from those
     of similar instruments used in our own culture.

3.   Folkways recording 8368 - Ragas - offers a very useful
     lecture-demonstration of Indian music. If you do not have
     or wish to buy the recording, a similar demonstration
     could be presented using a concert recording of improvised
     Indian music, preceded by a discussion of the specific
     ragas and talas that will be heard.

4.   If you can obtain them, visual examples of early Chinese
     and Japanese notation could contribute to a fascinating

comparison of another aspect of the music of East and West.

5. Students can obtain a better idea of Japanese "breath" rhythm if they attempt to clap out the rhythm used in an appropriate selection.

Discussion Questions

1. Because of the proliferation of phonograph records from the West, the field of ethnomusicology - the comparative study of the music of different cultures - has been described as the study of "disappearing" musical cultures. How true do you think this description will prove to be?

2. In what ways does the music of sub-Saharan African and that of the American Indian resemble Anglo-American folk music?

3. Within the last few decades, the music of India has become relatively popular in the United States, with large sales of records by such artists as Ravi Shankar. Why has so much interest been focused on Indian music, rather than on Chinese or Japanese music?

4. Which of the five musical styles discussed in Chapter 29 do you like best? Why?

5. As noted in Chapter 29, group composition has been favored in China in recent years. How feasible does such a system seem to you? How might it be implemented?

Listening Questions

Because the choice of non-Western recordings is likely to vary greatly from one record library to another, no specific listening questions have been included in Chapter 29. However, the following suggestions may prove useful:

1. Students can be asked to identify cultures while listening to representative but unfamiliar works from each of the five areas.

2. Questions involving categories of instruments heard in non-Western music can serve to reinforce understanding of timbre in general as well as the specific cultures involved.

3. If class coverage has included in-depth consideration of the music of India, listening questions involving the treatment of ragas and talas might be useful.

ANSWERS TO OBJECTIVE TEST (p. 189=191)

841. b 842. c 843. d 844. a 845. c 846. b 847. c 848. d
849. a 850. b 851. d 852. a 853. c 854. d 855. b
856. b 857. a 858. d 859. b 860. a

ANSWERS TO COMPLETION TEST (p. 191   )

861. dance 862. daily life 863. orchestras 864. short
melodic 865. rhythmic polyphony 866. wide
867. meaningless 868. owned 869. ragas 870. opera

CHAPTER 1   MELODY AND RHYTHM

1. Music is essentially sound organized within
   a. measures.
   b. movements.
   c. space.
   d. time.

2. We tend to hear a melody as a series of
   a. steps.
   b. phrases.
   c. rhythms.
   d. measures.

3. The position of a note on the staff indicates its
   a. duration.
   b. quality.
   c. pitch.
   d. intensity.

4. The overall speed of a piece is called its
   a. tempo.
   b. rhythm.
   c. movement.
   d. pulse.

5. A disjunct melody moves in
   a. halting rhythm.
   b. small steps.
   c. large leaps.
   d. short phrases.

6. The number of sound vibrations per second determines
   a. pulse.
   b. volume.
   c. duration.
   d. pitch.

7. The reular pattern of accented and unaccented beats is called
   a. meter.
   b. pulse.
   c. movement.
   d. rhythm.

8. A movement named for the old courtly dance it resembles is a(n)
   a. presto.
   b. menuetto.
   c. allegro.
   d. largo.

9. An oscillograph records fluctuations in
   a. duration.
   b. volume.
   c. pulse.
   d. vibration.

10. Rhythm generally falls into patterns of
    a. long and short notes.
    b. loud and soft notes.
    c. high and low notes.
    d. repeated notes.

11. The basic unit of meter is the
    a. measure.
    b. tempo.
    c. accent.
    d. rhythmic pattern.

12. Which of the following is <u>not</u> a tempo marking?
    a. lento   c. diminuendo
    b. presto   d. andante

13. A composer wishing to make use of syncopation would
    a. use a variety of meters.
    b. use a variety of rhythmic patterns.
    c. put an unaccented tone on a normally strong beat.
    d. put an accented tone on a normally weak beat.

14. A ritardando changes the
    a. rhythm.   c. meter.
    b. tempo.   d. pitch.

15. A measure in triple meter contains three
    a. accents.   c. beats.
    b. pitches.   d. notes.

16. A very fast movement might be marked
    a. poco accelerando.   c. adagio ma non troppo.
    b. allegro molto.   d. più moderato.

17. Until this century, composers generally avoided frequent changes of
    a. meter.   c. melody.
    b. tempo.   d. rhythm.

18. The strongest characteristic of a march is
    a. syncopation.   c. duple meter.
    b. disjunct melody.   d. broad tempo.

19. Structure in music is basically determined by
    a. the period in which the composer lived.
    b. the use of new and repeated elements.
    c. the purpose for which the music was intended.
    d. our expectations for the music.

20. A quickening of pace is called a(n)
    a. crescendo.   c. ritardando.
    b. prestissimo.   d. accelerando.

21. Pitches are thought of as an _____ or _____ movement.

22. Melodic structure usually has a _____, _____, and an _____ .

23. Rhythms are also found in _____ .

24. When music is played in absolutely strict meter the
    _____ impact of music is diminished.

25. Musical tempo markings are traditionally written in
    _____.

26. Prestissimo is _____ _____, while large is
    _____ _____.

27. Molto means _____.

28. Subdivision usually consists of dividing the beat into
    _____ notes.

29. The organizing principle in music is the _____.

30. Triple meter swings in _____, while duple swings
    in _____.

31. The most important element of music's vertical dimension is
    a.   melody.   c.   polyphony.
    b.   harmony.   d.   monophony.

32. Within an octave, how many different tones are available
    to the composer?
    a.   seven   c.   twelve
    b.   eight   d.   thirteen

33. Triads can be constructed by playing any three
    a.   consecutive tones of the chromatic scale.
    b.   consecutive tones of the major scale.
    c.   alternate tones of the chromatic scale.
    d.   alternate tones of the major scale.

34. The note of the major scale that pushes most strongly
    toward another note is the
    a.   first.   c.   fifth.
    b.   fourth.   d.   seventh.

35. Which of the following chords is a triad?
    a.   3-5-7   c.   1-4-5
    b.   2-5-8   d.   4-6-3

36. In a major tonality, the dominant triad will be
    a.   1-3-5   c.   5-7-2
    b.   4-6-8   d.   7-2-4

37. In the key of C major (C-D-E-F-G-A-B-C), the tonic chord
    will contain the note
    a.   F.   c.   G.
    b.   D.   d.   B.

38. The strongest resolution in Western music is the
    a.   "Amen" cadence.   c.   plagal cadence.
    b.   deceptive cadence.   d.   authentic cadence.

39. Which of the following progressions is not considered a
    resolution?
    a.   1-2   c.   IV-I
    b.   7-8   d.   V-I

40. The subdominant chord is based upon which note of the scale?
    a.   the second   c.   the fifth
    b.   the fourth   d.   the seventh

41. In the key of G major (G-A-B-C-D-E-F#-G), C# would be called
    a. the subdominant.   c. an accidental.
    b. a modulation.   d. an inversion.

42. The ear, hearing the dominant chord, expects the next chord to be
    a. I.   c. V.
    b. IV.   d. VI.

43. A tonal realignment that leads the ear to accept a new tonic is called a(n)
    a. accidental.   c. dissonance.
    b. inversion.   d. modulation.

44. The higher tone of the octave has a frequency of vibration that is
    a. one-half that of the lower note.
    b. the same as that of the lower note.
    c. twice that of the lower note.
    d. four times that of the lower note.

45. The dramatic interest of music is most enhanced by
    a. parallel counterpoint. c. octave duplication.
    b. modulation.   d. inversion.

46. In a plagal cadence, the resolution is
    a. IV-I.   c. V-I.
    b. I-IV.   d. V-IV.

47. Which of the following triads is inverted?
    a. 6-8-3   c. 7-2-4
    b. 5-7-2   d. 3-5-8

48. The texture of a composition depends on the particular way in which
    a. melodic and harmonic elements are interwoven.
    b. performing groups are set against each other.
    c. melodies are varied and developed.
    d. chords are inverted and arpeggiated.

49. In modern Western music
    a. texture generally remains constant throughout a composition.
    b. texture often changes during a composition.
    c. homophonic texture is rare, since it tends to become monotonous.
    d. polyphonic or contrapuntal texture is a thing of the past.

50. When the tones of a chord are played successively, they
    are said to be
    a. inverted.   c. arpeggiated.
    b. monophonic.   d. polyphonic.

51. Harmony is thought to have begun in the _____ century.

52. Harmony that centers around one note is called _____.

53. Consonant chords are described as _____ and
    _____.

54. If music is to express a full range of human emotions,
    _____ and _____ are necessary.

55. The scale used in Western music is called the _____
    scale.

56. A shifting of one tonic to a new tonic tone is called
    a _____.

57. The simplest kind of musical texture is _____.

58. A melody accompanied by chords is called _____
    texture.

59. Harmony is produced with the sounding of _____ or
    _____ tones at the same time.

60. One instrument that can play arpeggios easily is the
    _____.

CHAPTER 3   TIMBRE AND DYNAMICS

61. A person with a large larynx and -ong vocal chords is likely to have a
    a. rich, mellow voice.   c. low-pitched voice.
    b. hoarse, gravelly voice.   d. high-pitched voice.

62. Which of the following instruments would be most likely to appear in a modern orchestra?
    a. contrabassoon   c. recorder
    b. oboe d'amore   d. synthesizer

63. The indication for a gradual increase in volume is
    a. sf.   c. crescendo.
    b. fp.   d. diminuendo.

64. The musical instrument that varies most in timbre from one culture to another is the
    a. flute.   c. drum.
    b. harp.   d. human voice.

65. The characteristic qualities of a sound are called its
    a. texture.   c. technique.
    b. timbre.   d. tonality.

66. Percussion instruments in which the whole body of the instrument vibrates to produce the sound are known as
    a. idiophones.   c. vibraphones.
    b. membranophones.   d. aerophones.

67. Each of the brass instruments has
    a. at least one reed.   c. valves.
    b. a olido.   d. a flared bell

68. The most recently developed of the major keyboard instruments is the
    a. organ.   c. piano.
    b. harpichord.   d. clavichord.

69. Generally, one can expect that the shorter the vibrating string, the
    a. higher the sound.   c. softer the sound.
    b. lower the sound.   d. louder the sound.

70. A musical device that tends to generate excitement is called a
    a. ritardando.   c. diminuendo.
    b. decrescendo.   d. sforzando.

71. When a woodwind player covers one of more of the finger holes on the instrument, the result is
    a. shortening of the air column and a higher tone.
    b. lengthening of the air column and a lower tone.
    c. lengthening of the air column and a higher tone.
    d. cut off of the vibrations and a stopping of the sound.

72. An English horn is a(n)
    a. chordophone.
    b. wood aerophone.
    c. brass aerophone.
    d. idiophone.

73. An instrument that lacks rapid flexibility in dynamics is the
    a. clarinet.
    b. cello.
    c. harpsichord.
    d. bass drum.

74. Which of the following is not an idiophone?
    a. gong
    b. triangle
    c. cymbal
    d. bass drum

75. Which of the following is a single-reed instrument?
    a. clarinet
    b. oboe
    c. English horn
    d. bassoon

76. The highest ordinary male voice is the
    a. alto.
    b. contralto.
    c. tenor.
    d. baritone.

77. An instrument that cannot be played without electricity is the
    a. guitar.
    b. organ.
    c. recorder.
    d. synthesizer.

78. From highest to lowest, the brass instruments of the modern orchestra are
    a. horn, trumpet, trombone, tuba.
    b. trumpet, horn, trombone, tuba.
    c. trumpet, trombone, horn, tuba
    d. trombone, trumpet, horn, tuba

79. From softest to loudest, four of the most common dynamic markings are
    a. p, mp, mf, f.
    b. mp, p, f, mf.
    c. p, mp, f, mf.
    d. mp, p, mf, f.

80. An orchestral melody most freqently appears in the
    a. piano
    b. brass.
    c. woodwinds.
    d. strings.

81. More than likely, the first musical instruments were the
    _____ _____.

82. The highest range of female voices is called _____.

83. The term which describes a violinist plucking the strings
    of his instrument is called _____.

84. Wind instruments are usually made of _____ or _____.

85. The four families of instruments are _____, _____,
    _____ and _____.

86. The instrument that was developed for use in worship is
    called the _____ _____.

87. Dynamics are different _____ in sound.

88. Pianissimo means _____ _____.

89. Forte means _____.

90. An increase in volume is defined as _____.

91. The form of most popular and folk songs is
    a. strophic.
    c. ternary.
    b. binary.
    d. theme and variations.

92. Most marches are in
    a. strophic form.
    c. ternary form.
    b. binary form.
    d. sonata form.

93. The approximate dates of the Baroque era are
    a. 1450-1600.
    c. 1600-1750.
    b. 1500-1650.
    d. 1650-1800.

94. The two most fundamental principles of musical form are
    a. repetition and similarity.
    b. repetition and contrast.
    c. theme and development.
    d. theme and variations.

95. The shortest units of melody are
    a. motives.
    c. phrases.
    b. themes.
    d. measures.

96. The individual sections within each stanza of "The Star-Spangled Banner" are best represented as
    a. ABA.
    c. AABC.
    b. AABB.
    d. ABCD.

97. The ABA pattern represents
    a. binary form.
    c. rondo form.
    b. ternary form.
    d. strophic form.

98. The trend during the late eighteenth-century Classical era was toward
    a. simpler forms.
    c. freer forms.
    b. more elaborate forms.
    d. poetic forms.

99. The oldest of the following forms is the
    a. sonata.
    c. rondo.
    b. strophic.
    d. ritornello.

100. In a composition in ABA form, we expect to hear three sections, with the second section
    a. repeating the first.
    b. differing significantly from the first.
    c. acting as a development of the first.
    d. presenting a variation of the first.

101. Binary form is not often readily apparent to the listener because
    a. the separation of sections is usually not clear-cut.
    b. there is usually little difference between sections.
    c. the B section is always shorter than the A section.
    d. there is no sense of large-scale repetition.

102. A composition that always includes one or more singers is a
    a. symphonic poem.
    b. rhapsody.
    c. cantata.
    d. overture.

103. The year 1815 represents the
    a. high point of the Classical era.
    b. approximate end of the Classical era.
    c. precise beginning of the Romantic era.
    d. midpoint of the Romantic era.

104. Of the following listings of the structural units of form, which ranges from smallest to largest?
    a. motive, phrase, melody, section
    b. motive, melody, phrase, section
    c. phrase, motive, melody, section
    d. phrase, melody, motive, section

105. Dutch composer Jan Sweelinck, who lived from 1562 to 1621, would have done most of his composing during the
    a. transition from the Medieval to the Renaissance period.
    b. midpoint of the Renaissance period.
    c. transition from the Renaissance to the Baroque period.
    d. height of the Baroque period.

106. The form A - A^1 - A^2 - A^3 - etc. would be most likely to occur in
    a. Sousa's Stars and Stripes Forever.
    b. Brahms' Variations on a Theme by Haydn.
    c. Vaughan Williams' English Folk Songs.
    d. Schubert's Minuet, D. 85.

107. The closest musical analogy to the plot of a drama is
    a. technique.
    b. theme.
    c. style.
    d. form.

108. Muiscal form in an unfamiliar work is most apparent at the
    a. outset
    b. end.
    c. beginning of a contrasting section.
    d. beginning of the final section.

109. Strophic form presents the same or similar music for each text
    a. stanza.   c. line.
    b. phrase.   d. sentence.

110. The ritornello form developed in the seventeenth century, thus making it a
    a. Medieval form.   c. Baroque form.
    b. Renaissance form.   d. Classical form.

111. The overall design of a piece of music is called _____.

112. The two most fundamental principles of musical form are _____ and _____.

113. When the same music is repeated for each stanza the form is called _____.

114. Forms that do not fall into clear sectional patterns can be defined as _____ _____.

115. Compositional forms for individual solo singer and piano are called _____.

116. A B A C A D is called _____ form.

117. Extended orchestral forms are called _____.

118. The sonata form was developed by the late _____ century.

119. A movement is a _____ of a symphony.

120. The ritornello form evolved in the _____ century.

CHAPTER 5   MUSICAL NOTATION

121. A chromatic scale has how many notes between E and A?
  a. two   c. four
  b. three   d. five

122. Unlike the major scale, the minor scale has a half step between the
  a. first and second notes. c. third and fourth notes.
  b. second and third notes. d. fourth and fifth notes.

123. The middle line of the bass clef represents the note
  a. A.   c. C.
  b. B.   d. D.

124. The key of G has the same number of sharps as the key of
  a. B minor.   c. E minor.
  b. A minor.   d. G minor.

125. The key of D major has
  a. two sharps.   c. one sharp.
  b. two flats.   d. one flat.

126. In $\frac{4}{4}$ time, an eighth note will represent
  a. one beat.   c. one-quarter beat.
  b. one-half beat.   d. one-eighth beat.

127. The sign ¢ does not represent
  a. common time.   c. alla breve.
  b. cut time.   d. $\frac{2}{2}$ meter.

128. The division into measures is shown by
  a. staff lines.   c. bar lines.
  b. measure lines.   d. ledger lines.

129. The relative minor of B♭ major is
  a. D minor.   c. B♭ minor.
  b. G minor.   d. D♭ minor.

130. A C clef centered upon the fourth line of the staff is called a(n)
  a. treble clef.   c. tenor clef.
  b. alto clef.   d. bass clef.

131. B minor is the relative minor of
  a. B major.   c. G major.
  b. B♭ major.   d. D major.

132. Which of the following pairs of notes would <u>not</u> sound the same when played on the piano?
   a. B# and C♭   c. B♭ and A#
   b. G# and A♭   d. C# and D♭

133. The F clef is also known as the
   a. treble clef.   c. tenor clef.
   b. alto clef.   d. bass clef.

134. A 3/4 measure containing a dotted quarter note and an eighth rest may also contain
   a. another dotted quarter note.
   b. two eighth notes.
   c. four eighth notes.
   d. six sixteenth notes.

135. If middle C is to be located on the ledger line immediately below the staff, it is necessary to use the
   a. alto clef.   c. treble clef.
   b. tenor clef.   d. bass clef.

136. If a whole note represents four beats, a dotted half note will represent
   a. two beats.   c. four beats.
   b. three beats.   d. six beats.

137. Which of the following would be played on a black key of the piano?
   a. C#   c. E#
   b. F♭   d. B#

138. The great staff uses both the
   a. treble and alto clefs.   c. tenor and bass clefs.
   b. alto and bass clefs.   d. treble and bass clefs.

139. The C an octave above middle C falls in the
   a. alto clef.   c. treble clef.
   b. tenor clef.   d. bass clef.

140. The upper number of the time signature indicates
   a. which note has the value of one beat.
   b. the number of beats in a measure.
   c. the number of accents in a measure.
   d. the number of possible notes in a measure.

141. A series of five horizontal lines with four spaces in between is called a _____.

142. A treble clef is also called a _____ clef.

143. An F clef is also called a _____ clef.

144. The flat sign (♭) lowers the pitch by a _____-step.

145. Periods of silence are called _____.

146. Measures are divided by _____ _____.

147. The meter signature designates how many _____ are in each measure.

148. A sign that cancels a sharp (#) or flat (♭) sign is called a _____ sign.

149. A curved line that connects two alike pitches together is called a _____.

150. A curved line that connects two unlike pitches together is called a _____.

151. The two types of texts in the Mass liturgy are the
    a. Introit and Ordinary.   c. Gospel and Communion.
    b. Proper and Communion.   d. Ordinary and Proper.

152. The Medieval modes make use of how many different scale
    patterns?
    a. two   c. six
    b. four   d. sixteen

153. Probably the foremost composer of the French <u>Ars Nova</u> was
    a. Guillaume de Machaut.   c. Leonin.
    b. Perotin.   d. Bernart de Ventadorn.

154. Polyphony is best defined as music
    a. played by more than one instrument.
    b. sung by more than one voice.
    c. of more than one line sung at a time.
    d. sung by opposing choirs.

155. Medieval Church hymns were usually <u>not</u>
    a. sung by the congregation.
    b. based on folk songs.
    c. in strophic form.
    d. derived from chant.

156. Plainchant that uses many notes for each syllable of text
    is called
    a. syllabic.   c. Gregorian.
    b. melismatic.   d. plagal.

157. Leonin wrote in two styles -
    a. sacred and secular.
    b. homophonic and polyphonic.
    c. accompanied song and plainchant.
    d. organum and discantus.

158. Each mode occurs in two different versions, the authentic
    and the
    a. plagal.   c. major.
    b. dominant.   d. minor.

159. The practice of giving the tenor part an increasingly
    active role led to the development of the
    a. motet.   c. discantus style.
    b. madrigal.   d. ars nova.

160. The central service in Christian liturgical worship is
    a. the Mass.   c. Vespers.
    b. the Divine Office.   d. Matins.

161. The term "ars nova" was used in the title of a treatise by
    a. Guillaume de Machaut.   c. Perotin.
    b. Philippe de Vitry.   d. Leonin.

162. A group of singers who fourished a little later than the
    troubadours, and who sang in the northern French dialect,
    were the
    a. jongleurs.   c. Minnesingers.
    b. minstrels.   d. trouvères.

163. Religious music in the Middle Ages was almost entirely
    a. instrumental.   c. melismatic.
    b. vocal.   d. accompanied.

164. How many Medieval Church modes were there?
    a. two   c. eight
    b. four   d. sixteen

165. The Ars Nova style was not characterized by
    a. rhythmic simplicity.   c. triple meter.
    b. isorhythm.   d. duple meter.

166. The part of the Mass for which the text remains the same
    but the music varies is the
    a. Offertory.   c. Proper.
    b. Communion.   d. Ordinary.

167. The earliest type of polyphony was known as
    a. conductus.   c. organum.
    b. Gregorian chant.   d. discantus.

168. A practice in the polyphonic music of the thirteenth
    century that contributed to the development of the motet
    involved
    a. using more than one mode in a song.
    b. adding new texts to the upper lines.
    c. combining two ore more overlapping rhythms.
    d. using Greek melodies as a basis for secular songs.

169. In Leonin's polyphony, the original line of plainchant,
    presented in long notes, is called the
    a. tenor.   c. duplum.
    b. bass.   d. organum.

170. Bernart de Ventadorn was a
    a. Notre Dame choirmaster.
    b. successor of Leonin.
    c. twelfth-century French troubadour.
    d. fourteenth-century French troubadour.

171. The Medieval Period lasted _____ centuries.

172. A church service before the evening meal is called the
    _____ service.

173. The early music written for the Mass is called _____.

174. Leonin was associated with the School of _____ _____.

175. Tempus perfectum is _____ _____.

176. In fourteenth-century France music and poetry were
    considered _____ _____.

177. Two different kinds of texts used in the Mass were
    _____ and _____.

178. The _____ Medieval mode developed into the familiar
    major scale.

179. Melodic styles of plain chant were written in _____,
    _____, and _____ types.

180. Organized metrical patterns were called _____ modes.

CHAPTER 7   RENAISSANCE MUSIC

181. The first printer of music was
    a. Petrucci.
    b. Marenzio.
    c. Attaignant.
    d. Dowland.

182. Which technique is <u>not</u> closely associated with canon?
    a. inversion
    b. modulation
    c. imitation
    d. augmentation

183. A chorale is essentially the same as a
    a. motet.
    b. madrigal.
    c. chant.
    d. hymn.

184. The Venetian style of composition is most closely identified with the name
    a. Gabrieli.
    b. Scarlatti.
    c. Monteverdi.
    d. Gesualdo.

185. The "fa-la-la" refrain was a typical device of the English
    a. ayre.
    b. song.
    c. ballett.
    d. madrigal.

186. The early development of the Italian madrigal was influenced by the chordal, syllabic Italian part song known as the
    a. virelai.
    b. frottola.
    c. canzona.
    d. caccia.

187. Madrigals with a strongly personal style, featuring juxtaposition of unrelated chords, were composed in the late sixteenth century by
    a. Petrucci.
    b. Ockeghem.
    c. Morley.
    d. Gesualdo.

188. A grouping of recorders, viols, lutes, and sackbuts would most accurately be called a
    a. consort.
    b. broken consort.
    c. haut consort.
    d. bas consort.

189. By the mid-sixteenth century, the Italian madrigal normally contained how many voices?
    a. three
    b. four
    c. five
    d. six

190. The Venetian style of the late Renaissance typically made use of
    a. huge choral groups.
    b. an informal song style with simple melodies.
    c. a rich, closely knit imitative style.
    d. contrasting groups of voices and instruments.

191. Which of the following does not describe the style of Palestrina?
    a. highly subjective, emotional, and chromatic
    b. abundant use of contrapuntal imitation
    c. overlapping phrases with infrequent cadences
    d. careful and conservative use of dissonance

192. A sackbut is what kind of instrument?
    a. string   c. percussion
    b. wind   d. keyboard

193. The hymn tune "Ein' feste Burg ist unser Gott" was probably composed by
    a. Isaac.   c. Luther.
    b. Ockeghem.   d. Bach.

194. Which of the following Renaissance forms was a vocal composition?
    a. ballett   c. galliard
    b. ricercar   d. fantasia

195. The composer who most closely adhered to the style advocated by the Council of Trent was
    a. Gesualdo.   c. Monteverdi.
    b. Mosley.   d. Palestrina.

196. During the Renaissance, the standard number of parts for a polyphonic work was generally
    a. two.   c. four.
    b. three.   d. six.

197. Roland de Lassus is best known for his
    a. richly contrapuntal Masses.
    b. accompanied part songs.
    c. popular instrumental pieces.
    d. highly expressive motets.

198. During the Elizabethan period, the chief instrument used by amateurs and professionals for informal accompaniment of song was the
    a. dulcimer.   c. harpsichord.
    b. lute.   d. harp.

199. Monteverdi's "Si ch'io vorrei morire" is
    a. homophonic and contrapuntal.
    b. monophonic and contrapuntal.
    c. monophonic and homophonic.
    d. monophonic, homophonic, and contrapuntal.

200. The form of Palestrina's Kyrie is
    a. AB.   c. ABC.
    b. ABA.   d. ABCD.

201. The texture of Renaissance music is mainly _____.

202. The _____ became important in the Lutheran Protestant church service.

203. The composer who became the most celebrated musician in Europe during this lifetime was _____.

204. The Venetian School composers encouraged the use of _____.

205. The creative climate of the Renaissance was called _____.

206. Palestrina spent his career in _____.

207. The art of music printing began with _____.

208. Thomas Morley was among the most popular composers of English _____.

209. English ballets can be recognized by their _____ refrains.

210. Renaissance instruments were grouped in families called _____.

211. Strange, distorted figures were a feature of the paintings of
    a. Wölfflin.
    b. El Greco.
    c. Leeuwenhoek.
    d. Rembrandt.

212. Compared to the music of the Renaissance, Baroque music
    a. placed greater stress upon vocal music.
    b. tended more toward single-movement works.
    c. used more elaborate melodic ornamentation.
    d. was stricter in its treatment of dissonance.

213. A declamatory style, free rhythm, and simple melody were most characteristic of Baroque
    a. recitatives.
    b. arias.
    c. ariosos.
    d. concertatos.

214. Which of the following was not an innovation of the Baroque era?
    a. terraced dynamics
    b. equal temperament
    c. major-minor harmony
    d. imitative counterpoint

215. In the early decades of the Baroque era, orchestras were chiefly associated with
    a. church music.
    b. court music.
    c. opera.
    d. chamber music.

216. The term "concertato" refers to
    a. the Florentine group that developed the monodic style.
    b. a wooden instrument of soft tone that gradually fell into disuse.
    c. improvised harmonic support for a melody.
    d. a style that pitted performing groups against one another.

217. Monteverdi called the polyphonic style of the Renaissance the
    a. prima prattica.
    b. secunda prattica.
    c. stile rappresentativo.
    d. bel canto.

218. The texture of music written in basso continuo style is generally
    a. polyphonic.
    b. homophonic.
    c. monophonic.
    d. monodic.

219. Baroque organ music reached its highest development in
    a. England.
    b. Italy.
    c. France.
    d. Germany.

220. Which of the following Baroque instrumental compositions was always in one movement?
a. concerto
b. sonata
c. fugue
d. suite

221. The Baroque period in music covers approximately the years
a. 1550-1650.
b. 1600-1750.
c. 1650-1780.
d. 1700-1850.

222. The earliest creative center of Baroque music was
a. Italy.
b. Spain.
c. Germany.
d. France.

223. The great Baroque composer Georg Friedrich Handel
a. lived in Germany all his life.
b. went blind before his death.
c. was born in the same year as Monteverdi.
d. was chiefly interested in polyphony.

224. "Realization" refers particularly to the Baroque use of
a. basso continuo.
b. terraced dynamics.
c. modulation.
d. affections.

225. The opera Orfeo was written by
a. Bach.
b. Corelli.
c. Handel.
d. Monteverdi.

226. Larger compositions were made possible by the use of
a. figured bass.
b. terraced dynamics.
c. modulation.
d. chordal progression.

227. Which of the following was not one of the favored instruments of the Baroque period?
a. harpsichord
b. clavichord
c. piano
d. organ

228. The type of composition not new in the Baroque era was the
a. concerto.
b. Mass.
c. sonata.
d. oratorio.

229. The stile rappresentativo, with its emphasis on monody, developed out of
a. the doctrine of the affections.
b. the Italian madrigal form.
c. the bel canto style.
d. an interest in Greek drama.

230. Equal temperament had the greatest effect upon
a. harmony.
b. meter.
c. rhythm.
d. dynamics.

231. The absolutist state par excellence during the early 1600s was _____.

232. The imbalance of bodily fluids was called the _____ ____ ____ _____.

233. One ornamental device that developed in the Baroque Age was the _____.

234. Bel Canto style means to sing in a _____ manner.

235. Dissonance during the Baroque era was _____.

236. Imitative counterpoint is called _____.

237. Figured bass was called _____ _____.

238. _____ was a new vocal form that developed during the Baroque period.

239. Early religious music in America was found in the _____ _____ colonies.

240. A group of learned men during the early Baroque era were called the _____.

241. Monteverdi's continuo madrigal style
    a. allowed for freer use of dissonance.
    b. gave greater prominence to the inner voices.
    c. added more voices to those used in the Renaissance.
    d. added basso continuo to the Renaissance madrigal, but left it otherwise unchanged.

242. Opera was a type of music-drama that evolved in the
    a. late sixteenth century.
    b. early seventeenth century.
    c. late seventeenth century.
    d. early eighteenth century.

243. The da capo aria has the form
    a. AB.   c. AA^1
    b. ABC.   d. ABA^1.

244. The Neapolitan opera style was essentially
    a. homophonic.   c. polyphonic.
    b. monodic.   d. monophonic.

245. The Baroque Missa brevis included the
    a. Sanctus.   c. Gloria.
    b. Credo.   d. Agnus Dei.

246. In his choruses, Handel was apt to emphasize climaxes with the use of
    a. homophonic chordal passages.
    b. imitative polyphonic passages.
    c. striking modulations.
    d. chromaticism.

247. The opera Euridice, by Caccini and Peri, was written in the
    a. Neapolitan style.   c. monodic style.
    b. opera buffa style.   d. French style.

248. Which of the following was not typical of the bel canto style of opera in the mid-seventeenth century?
    a. light, lyrical melodies and smooth rhythms
    b. complex harmonies of striking originality
    c. a growing importance of the bass line, leading toward the reintroduction of contrapuntal techniques
    d. orchestral accompaniment

249. An aria that makes use of a constantly repeating bass line is the
   a. strophic-bass aria.
   b. ostinato aria.
   c. da capo aria.
   d. basso continuo aria.

250. The composer usually regarded as the founder of Neopolitan opera was
   a. Monteverdi.
   b. Alessandro Scarlatti.
   c. Domenico Scarlatti.
   d. Peri.

251. Oratorios differ from opera in that
   a. oratorios are seldom staged.
   b. oratorios are always performed in churches.
   c. operas never deal with biblical subjects.
   d. operas never use the chorus for dramatic purposes.

252. In Bach's cantatas, a chorale tune was most likely to appear in
   a. the opening movement.
   b. all movements.
   c. all choral movements.
   d. the last movement.

253. The Neapolitan opera style arose in the
   a. early seventeenth century.
   b. mid-seventeenth century.
   c. late seventeenth century.
   d. early eighteenth century.

254. The expression of complex emotions would be least likely to appear in a(n)
   a. recitativo accompagnato.
   b. recitativo secco.
   c. arioso.
   d. aria.

255. More than six hundred cantatas were composed by
   a. Alessandro Scarlatti.
   b. Schütz.
   c. Buxtehude.
   d. Bach.

256. Which of the following is not typical of the French operatic school?
   a. inclusion of long scenes, such as combats, processions, funerals, and other eye-pleasing spectacles
   b. compression of the overture into one allegro movement
   c. shorter, simpler arias that avoided virtuoso effects
   d. colorful and elaborate orchestration

257. The form of the Sanctus of Bach's Mass in B Minor is
   a. ABCB.
   b. ABCD.
   c. ABCBD.
   d. ABCDC.

130

258. Many of the early seventeenth century's leading composers wrote operas that were performed in the world's first public opera house in
a. Florence.
b. Rome.
c. Venice.
d. Naples.

259. Handel's operas display a thorough mastery of the
a. Neapolitan style.
b. Venetian style.
c. Florentine style.
d. Roman style.

260. The composer most instrumental in carrying out the transition from the Italian madrigal to the German sacred cantata was
a. Alessandro Scarlatti.
b. Schütz.
c. Buxtehude.
d. Bach.

261. The first Contino madrigals were written by _____.

262. Monteverdi wrote only _____ music.

263. _____ wrote Italian operas in England.

264. _____ brought English opera to greatness.

265. The opera Julius Caesar was written by _____.

266. An early composer of cantatas was _____.

267. The Mass became _____ _____ during the Baroque era.

268. Unlike Handel, Bach made his career entirely in _____.

269. _____ was the Italian composer who wrote French operas.

270. Opera buffa is _____ opera.

271. During the middle Baroque
  a. instrumental music began to emerge from its subordination to vocal music.
  b. contrapuntal music all but disappeared.
  c. there was a renewed interest in harmony based upon the Church modes.
  d. the predominance of French music was giving way to the Italian influence.

272. A typical Baroque composition consisting of a number of dance-like movements in the same or related keys was known as a
  a. sinfonia.   c. toccata.
  b. church sonata.   d. suite.

273. A trio sonata generally includes
  a. three melody instruments.
  b. two melody instruments and one basso continuo instrument.
  c. two melody instruments and two basso continuo instruments.
  d. one melody instrument and two basso continuo instruments.

274. Which of the following is not typical of the fugue?
  a. style brise   c. imitative counterpoint
  b. complex polyphony   d. modulation

275. Another name for a suite is
  a. sinfonia.   c. canzon da sonar.
  b. partita.   d. concerto grosso.

276. One of the great composers of both church and chamber sonatas was
  a. Lully.   c. Vivaldi.
  b. Bach.   d. Corelli.

277. Antonio Vivaldi wrote more than 450
  a. fugues.   c. concertos.
  b. suites.   d. sonatas.

278. The French overture was largely the creation of
  a. Rameau.   c. Lully.
  b. Couperin.   d. Alessandro Scarlatti.

279. Which of the following did <u>not</u> figure importantly in the evolution of the concerto?
  a. a renewed interest in instrumental polyphony and imitative counterpoint
  b. contrast between large and small groups
  c. major-minor harmony
  d. the idea of combining several short sections in a single composition

280. The evolution of the solo concerto and its unique structure are linked to the works of
  a. Corelli.   c. Bach.
  b. Torelli.   d. Vivaldi.

281. The pattern of sections in the Italian overture is
  a. slow - fast.   c. slow - fast - slow.
  b. fast - slow.   d. fast - slow - fast.

282. Numerous suites for harpsichord were composed by
  a. Corelli.   c. Domenico Scarlatti.
  b. Couperin.   d. Vivaldi.

283. Every fugue must have
  a. a prelude.   c. an exposition.
  b. a countersubject. d. four voices.

284. The term "sinfonia" came to mean
  a. the instrumental introduction or interludes of a vocal work.
  b. a short symphony in one or two movements.
  c. a short keyboard composition played by small chamber orchestra.
  d. a succession of dancelike movements similar to the suite.

285. Over six hundred solo sonatas for harpsichord were written by
  a. Vivaldi.   c. Alessandro Scarlatti.
  b. Corelli.   d. Domenico Scarlatti.

286. Which of the following is usually credited with having created the concerto grosso?
  a. Corelli   c. Domenico Scarlatti
  b. Vivaldi   d. Lully

287. The most important type of orchestral composition developed during the Baroque period was the
  a. symphony.   c. overture.
  b. sinfonia.   d. concerto.

288. The concertino in Corelli's concerti grossi usually consisted of
    a. violin and cello.
    b. two violins and one cello.
    c. two violins, one cello, and keyboard instrument.
    d. two violins, one viola, and one cello.

289. Which of the following was not typical of the German suite style?
    a. A more unified style of composition than that of the French suites
    b. An increasing tendency to abandon set dance forms such as the allemande, courante, and sarabande
    c. Increased use of counterpoint
    d. The introduction of wind instruments into the string ensemble

290. In a fugue, sections of freely invented counterpoint are called
    a. expositions.   c. countersubjects.
    b. subjects.   d. episodes.

291. Stile rappresentativo had its emphasis on _____ _____ and _____ .

292. The concertato style had its emphasis on _____ _____ .

293. The term tutti means _____ .

294. Ripieno, solo form is an example of the _____ principle.

295. The abbreviation "Op." stands for _____ .

296. A repetition of melodic material at increasingly higher pitches is an example of _____ .

297. The pattern of sections in French overture is _____ .

298. The French dances were written for _____ instruments.

299. The structure of the solo keyboard suites was based on the _____ .

300. _____ was an early composer or toccatas.

CHAPTER 11   INTRODUCTION TO CLASSICAL MUSICAL STYLES

301. If a movement in Classical music opens in a major key, it will most likely modulate to the
   a. dominant.
   c. subdominant.
   b. relative major.
   d. relative minor.

302. Classical music is
   a. based upon models of ancient Greek and Roman music.
   b. related in spirit to ancient artistic ideals.
   c. based upon models of Renaissance music.
   d. simpler in all respects than Baroque music.

303. The dominating melody of a work or movement is usually called its
   a. subject.
   c. motive.
   b. exposition.
   d. theme.

304. The scale of C minor has a half step
   a. above E^b.
   c. above F.
   b. below E^b.
   d. below F.

305. The Mannheim orchestra was particularly known for its
   a. connection with the Empfindsamer Stil.
   b. connection with the Rococo style.
   c. mastery of terraced dynamics.
   d. mastery of varied dynamic effects.

306. The section of sonata form most often repeated is the
   a. exposition.
   c. recapitulation.
   b. development.
   d. coda.

307. Carl Philipp Emanuel Bach
   a. composed very much in the style of his father.
   b. helped create the Empfindsamer Stil.
   c. helped create the Mannheim school of composition.
   d. was the first to use clarinets in an orchestral work.

308. Frequent modulation is most characteristic of the sonata form's
   a. introduction.
   c. development.
   b. exposition.
   d. recapitulation.

309. A key closely related to G major is
   a. D major.
   c. B^b major.
   b. F major.
   d. D^b major.

310. A movement in sonata form that begins in G minor is most likely to modulate to
   a. G major.
   c. D major.
   b. D minor.
   d. B^b major.

311. How many whole steps are there in the major scale?
    a. two   c. four
    b. three   d. five

312. Which of the following would <u>not</u> be considered a sonata cycle?
    a. a symphony   c. a concerto
    b. an overture   d. a string quartet

313. Much of the unity of Classical music derives from the
    a. regularity of its phrases.
    b. stress upon a single key.
    c. stress upon a single mode.
    d. small-scale orchestration.

314. The greatest advantage of the modern pianoforte over the harpsichord is its
    a. wider tonal range.
    b. gentler, quieter tone.
    c. percussive brilliance.
    d. greater dynamic flexibility.

315. "Sonata form" or "sonata-allegro form" denotes
    a. the overall form of the sonata cycle.
    b. the form of one or several movements within a sonata cycle.
    c. a form containing three themes and two main sections.
    d. a form stressing repeated development of a single theme.

316. The relative major of E minor is
    a. E major.   c. G major.
    b. C major.   d. D major.

317. Which of the following series of composers is arranged, in accordance with the Classical-Romantic continuum, from most Classical to most Romantic?
    a. C.P.E. Bach, Mozart, Brahms, Chopin
    b. Haydn, Berlioz, Beethoven, Liszt
    c. Mozart, Beethoven, Schubert, Brahms
    d. Beethoven, Berlioz, Schubert, Liszt

318. The Classical symphony orchestra did <u>not</u> generally include
    a. trombones.   c. horns.
    b. bassoons.   d. percussion instruments.

319. The dominant triad of a piece in B^b major is built on the note
    a. E^b.   c. G.
    b. F.   d. A^b.

320. In sonata form, the recapitulation is usually
    a. identical to the exposition.
    b. difficult to distinguish clearly from the development.
    c. based on the home key, with only brief excursions to related keys.
    d. in the relative major or minor key, with occasional references to the home key.

321. During the Classical period the Age of Reason soon passed into the _____ _____ _____.

322. During the music of the Classical age, a high degree of _____ and _____ is readily seen.

323. Classical music differed from that of the Baroque in its _____ organization of melodic material.

324. In Classical music, as in simple folk songs, melody is organized into regularly recurring _____.

325. A steady meter and a regularly recurring pulse generally characterizes the _____ style.

326. As the Classical style emerged in the mid-eighteenth century, the texture of music tended to be _____ and _____.

327. In the early Classical orchestra the _____ section was given most of the melodic material.

328. The piano forte was invented in _____.

329. The typical five-part Rondo form might be diagrammed as _____.

330. The singing school began around 1720 in _____.

331. Mozart lived from 1756 to
   a. 1784.   c. 1807.
   b. 1791.   d. 1815.

332. The rondo form was used most frequently in Classical
   symphonies for the
   a. opening movement.   c. minuet and trio.
   b. slow movement.   d. concluding movement.

333. In an andante movement, the tempo is
   a. very slow.   c. moderate.
   b. slow.   d. fast.

334. In Haydn's "Surprise" Symphony, the movement that
   immediately charmed London audiences and gave the symphony
   its name was the
   a. first.   c. third.
   b. second.   d. fourth.

335. Rapid scales and sequences are most likely to appear in a
   a. bridge passage.   c. second theme.
   b. variation.   d. trio section.

336. The symphony found its first great master in
   a. Beethoven.   c. Haydn.
   b. Stamitz.   d. Mozart.

337. The movement of Mozart's Symphony No. 40 in G Minor that
   begins with a rocket motive is the
   a. first.   c. third.
   b. second.   d. fourth.

338. In addition to the movements in sonata form, Haydn's
   "Surprise" Symphony and Mozart's Symphony No. 40 in G
   Minor both contain a movement in
   a. theme and variations form.
   b. ternary form.
   c. rondo form.
   d. sonata-rondo form.

339. Which of the following best represents a rondo form?
   a. ABACABA   c. A - A^1 - A^2 - A^3 - A^4
   b. AB   d. AABB

340. Mozart's Symphony No. 40 in G Minor uses sonata form in
   how many movements?
   a. one   c. three
   b. two   d. four

341. The composer whom Haydn acknowledged as the greatest of his time was
   a. Beethoven.
   b. C.P.E. Bach
   c. Stamitz.
   d. Mozart.

342. The trio section of a minuet-and-trio movement is usually characterized by
   a. lighter instrumentation.
   b. trio-sonata form.
   c. a change from triple to duple meter.
   d. quicker motion.

343. The opening theme of the first movement of Mozart's Symphony No. 40 in G Minor is not characterized by
   a. sequence.
   b. motivic repetition.
   c. primarily conjunct motion.
   d. primarily ascending motion.

344. In 1791, Haydn was commissioned by Johann Peter Salomon to compose and conduct what are now known as the
   a. Vienna Symphonies.
   b. London Symphonies.
   c. Surprise Symphonies.
   d. Esterházy Symphonies.

345. An introduction is found in the
   a. first movement of Haydn's "Surprise" Symphony.
   b. last movement of Haydn's "Surprise" Symphony.
   c. first movement of Mozart's Symphony No. 40 in G Minor.
   d. last movement of Mozart's Symphony No. 40 in G Minor.

346. Ludwig von Köchel
   a. was Mozart's teacher.
   b. was Mozart's patron.
   c. commissioned Mozart's last three symphonies.
   d. catalogued Mozart's works.

347. Which of the following was not used by Haydn in the theme and variations movement of his "Surprise" Symphony?
   a. dotted rhythm
   b. 3:1 rhythm
   c. theme inversion
   d. modal shift

348. A coda is a passage used
   a. at the beginning of a movement.
   b. between the exposition and the development.
   c. between the development and the recapitulation.
   d. at the end of a movement.

349. Mozart's career was characterized by
   a. the security and artistic encouragement he found in the patronage system.
   b. financial difficulties, emotional tension, and artistic insecurity.
   c. constant adulation and financial success.
   d. illness and eventual blindness.

350. The surprise of Haydn's "Surprise" Symphony is created mainly by
    a. dynamics.   c. rhythm.
    b. harmony.   d. meter.

351. While some of the early symphonies have only three movements,_____ movements soon became the standard number.

352. _____ was the first composer to allow folk music in his Classical compositions.

353. _____ wrote 104 symphonies plus many other works.

354. The form of Haydn's Symphony No. 94, 2nd movement is _____ and _____ .

355. The Classical period coincided with the rise of a strong _____ culture.

356. The two greatest composers of the Classical period were _____ and _____ .

357. Mozart's Symphony No. 41 is also known as the _____ symphony.

353. Beethoven's only opera was called _____ .

359. The Missa solemnis, a setting of the mass, was written by _____ .

360. The fourth movement of Beethoven's Ninth symphony contains _____ and _____ as well as orchestra.

361. Beethoven was born in
    a. Vienna.
    b. Salzburg.
    c. Heiligenstadt.
    d. Bonn.

362. The term "scherzo" comes from the Italian word for
    a. symphony.
    b. dance.
    c. joke.
    d. fast.

363. Beethoven's "Pastoral" Symphony is his
    a. Third Symphony.
    b. Sixth Symphony.
    c. Seventh Symphony.
    d. Ninth Symphony.

364. As a boy, Beethoven
    a. received a reasonably thorough general education.
    b. suffered the first awareness of inpending deafness.
    c. worked as first violinist in the court orchestra.
    d. worked as assistant organist at the Elector's court.

365. The symphony Beethoven conceived as a tribute to
    Napoleon was the
    a. third.
    b. fifth.
    c. seventh.
    d. ninth.

366. The opening motive of Beethoven's Symphony No. 5 in C
    Minor is later altered by the
    a. shortening of the first note.
    b. shortening of the last note.
    c. lengthening of the first note.
    d. lengthening of the last note.

367. Beethoven's father was a
    a. moderately well known and respected composer.
    b. highly talented and versatile musician.
    c. court singer of no great talent.
    d. well known violin virtuoso.

368. Beethoven's attitude toward the rules of composition in
    his time was essentially
    a. conservative.
    b. revolutionary.
    c. neutral.
    d. ambiguous.

369. When Beethoven first became concerned about his approach-
    ing deafness, he was living at
    a. Heiligenstadt.
    b. Salzburg.
    c. Bonn.
    d. Mannheim.

370. The most popular of Beethoven's symphonies is almost
certainly the
a. "Eroica."   c. fifth.
b. "Pastoral."   d. ninth.

371. Which of the following is not characteristic of
Beethoven's orchestration?
a. The strings are given a subordinate role
b. New instruments are added to the orchestra
c. The wind instruments are given more prominent melodic
roles
d. Various instruments exchange motives

372. In Vienna, Beethoven studied with
a. Waldstein.   c. Leopold Mozart.
b. Haydn.   d. Wolfgang Amadeus Mozart.

373. Soloists and a large choir join the orchestra for the
finale of Beethoven's
a. Third Symphony.   c. Seventh Symphony.
b. Sixth Symphony.   d. Ninth Symphony.

374. In Beethoven's Symphony No. 5 in C Minor, a transition
joins
a. the first and second movements.
b. the second and third movements.
c. the third and fourth movements.
d. all movements.

375. Which of the following is not typical of the scherzo form?
a. serious mood   c. triple meter
b. fast tempo   d. ternary form

376. The second movement of Beethoven's Fifth Symphony is in
a. sonata form.
b. theme and variations form.
c. rondo form.
d. scherzo form.

377. Beethoven introduced the trombone to the orchestra in his
Fifth Symphony's
a. first movement.   c. third movement.
b. second movement.   d. fourth movement.

378. Beethoven was probably the first composer who
a. used a single motivic idea in each movement of a
symphony.
b. used percussion instruments in the symphony orchestra.
c. divided the violin section into first and second
violins.
d. conducted his own music.

379. In the third movement of his Symphony No. 5 in C Minor, Beethoven gives an unusually prominent melodic role to the
a. trombones.
b. double basses.
c. contrabassoons.
d. horns.

380. Which of the following did Beethoven not include in his symphonies?
a. use of harp
b. use of choruses
c. use of five movements
d. use of vocal soloists

381. _____ was among the first musicians of common background to mix with the aristocracy on his own terms.

382. Beethoven's democratic ideals were rooted in the _____ _____.

383. "Fate knocking at the door" is an explanation of the motive for the _____ symphony.

384. Beethoven wrote _____ symphonies.

385. Beethoven's three different styles of writing were called _____, _____, and _____.

386. The text of Beethoven's Ninth symphony, 4th movement is based on Schiller's _____.

387. Before Beethoven's Ninth symphony, _____ forces had never been used in such a form.

388. _____ and _____ were the first composers to be paid for their compositions.

389. The _____ symphony has movement titles that sound like chapter titles in a novel.

390. _____ isolated Beethoven from society and turned him into a romantic figure.

CHAPTER 14   CONCERTOS OF MOZART
AND HIS CONTEMPORARIES

391. Mozart's Piano Concerto No. 17 is in the key of
    a. G minor.   c. C minor.
    b. G major.   d. C major.

392. The earliest Baroque concertos were written for
    a. harpsichord.   c. recorder.
    b. organ.   d. violin.

393. The first movement of a Classical concerto is usually in sonata form, but with a
    a. double introduction.   c. second development.
    b. second exposition.   d. second recapitulation.

394. Beethoven wrote how many piano concertos?
    a. five   c. nine
    b. seven   d. twenty-seven

395. The third movement of Mozart's Piano Concerto No. 17 is written in
    a. rondo form.   c. theme and variations form.
    b. sonata form.   d. minuet and trio form.

396. In general, compared to the Baroque concerto, the Classical concerto features a(n)
    a. enlarged orchestra.   c. enlarged concertino.
    b. smaller orchestra.   d. enlarged basso continuo.

397. The overall mood of the last movement of a Classical concerto is usually
    a. lyrical and spacious.   c. dramatic and intense.
    b. humorous and light.   d. lively and dancelike.

398. Mozart, as a boy, wrote concerto arrangements of some works by
    a. C.P.E. Bach.   c. Franz Josef Haydn.
    b. J.C. Bach.   d. Michael Haydn.

399. Beethoven's concertos illustrate his movement over the years toward
    a. deafness and despair.
    b. more complex polyphonic forms.
    c. a more Romantic style.
    d. a more abstract, less expressive style.

400. A written cadenza must ideally contain
a. virtuosic passages for solo instrument and orchestra.
b. remnants of all themes of the movement.
c. a lyrical segment.
d. a spirit of free improvisation.

401. In addition to his piano concertos, Beethoven wrote a solo concerto for
a. trumpet.   c. cello.
b. violin.   d. clarinet.

402. Which of the following most accurately describes the Classical concerto?
a. sonata cycle   c. sonata form
b. suite   d. concerto grosso

403. The aspect of Italian opera that most influenced the Classical concerto was the
a. recitative.   c. aria.
b. arioso.   d. chorus.

404. Which of the following is least typical of the Classical concerto?
a. contrast between movements
b. structural use of themes
c. structural use of tonality
d. subordination of orchestra to instrumental soloist

405. Beethoven wrote a "triple concerto" for
a. violin, cello, and piano.
b. viola, cello, and piano.
c. violin and two pianos.
d. two violins and piano.

406. In the theme and variations movement of his Piano Concerto No. 17, Mozart does not use a
a. 3:1 rhythmic variation.   c. solo piano variation.
b. minor mode variation.   d. coda.

407. The cadenza in Mozart's Piano Concerto No. 17 was
a. left to the discretion of the performer.
b. written out by the composer.
c. composed later by Köchel.
d. composed later by Beethoven.

408. Beethoven's Piano Concerto No. 5 in E♭ Major is known as the
a. "Emperor."   c. "Appassionata."
b. "Eroica."   d. "Moonlight."

409. The solo concerto of the Classical period developed from the
a. Classical symphony.   c. Baroque sonata.
b. Italian opera.   d. Baroque concerto.

410. Mozart wrote how many concertos?
a. about ten   c. more than forty
b. nearly thirty   d. more than one hundred

411. The Classical concerto is a _____ _____ between solo instrument and orchestra.

412. The earliest of the concertos was written for _____ and orchestra.

413. The concerto, the Classical style, was also influenced by the Italian _____.

414. A Classical concerto is almost always made up of _____ movements.

415. The second movement of a Classical concerto allows for much _____ on the part of a soloist.

416. Haydn's Concerto in F Major was written for _____, _____ solo instruments and strings.

417. The _____ usually announces the first theme in a Classical concerto.

418. The most common tempo pattern between movements of a Classical concerto is _____, _____, _____.

419. Ritornello means the _____ plays the theme.

420. The increased importance of the _____ part was to become a feature of Romantic concertos.

CHAPTER 15 CHAMBER MUSIC OF HAYDN, MOZART, AND BEETHOVEN

421. A chamber work achieves its effect through
    a. the scaling down of the emotional impact.
    b. the emphasis on one or two melodic instruments.
    c. the dialogue among individual instruments.
    d. its essentially consonant, tranquil harmonies.

422. The string quartet first took definite form in the compositions of
    a. Michael Haydn.
    b. Franz Josef Haydn.
    c. Mozart.
    d. Beethoven.

423. Beethoven wrote how many piano sonatas?
    a. ten
    b. sixteen
    c. thirty-two
    d. forty-five

424. A piano quintet generally includes
    a. five pianos.
    b. two violins.
    c. four violins.
    d. five string instruments.

425. The second movement of Haydn's String Quartet in C Major, Op. 76, No. 3 is in
    a. sonata form.
    b. theme and variations form.
    c. rondo form.
    d. ternary form.

426. Beethoven's "Pathétique" Sonata is in the key of
    a. C minor.
    b. C major.
    c. F minor.
    d. F major.

427. The basso continuo of the Baroque period was
    a. frequently retained in early Classical quartets.
    b. supplanted by piano accompaniment in most Classical quartets.
    c. taken over entirely by the cello in Classical quartets.
    d. gradually dropped during the Classical period.

428. The set of quartets of which Haydn's Quartet in C Major, Op. 76, No. 3 is a part includes how many other quartets?
    a. one
    b. five
    c. seven
    d. eleven

429. Which of the following is <u>not</u> true of Haydn's string quartets?
    a. They follow the structure of the sonata cycle.
    b. Sonata form is used in first movements.
    c. His later works became shorter and simpler.
    d. They usually contain four movements.

430. Haydn wrote how many string quartets?
    a. nine   c. over ninety
    b. over eighty   d. one hundred and four

431. Haydn's <u>Quartet in C Major</u>, Op. 76, No. 3, has how many movements in sonata form?
    a. one   c. three
    b. two   d. four

432. The Italian word indicating a singing style is
    a. staccato.   c. cantabile.
    b. toccata.   d. appassionata.

433. Which of the following is <u>not</u> true of chamber music in general?
    a. performed by a small group of players
    b. written for string ensembles only
    c. performed without a conductor
    d. each part performed by a single player

434. In the mature Classical string quartet, the melody
    a. is shared rather equally by all four instruments.
    b. is almost always given to the first violin.
    c. is shared rather equally by the two violins.
    d. is shared rather equally by the first violin and cello.

435. The epitome of the Classical piano sonata was reached in the works of
    a. Haydn.   c. Beethoven.
    b. Mozart.   d. Schubert.

436. The first melody of Haydn's <u>Quartet in C Major</u>, Op. 76, No. 3, is
    a. very lyrical.   c. played first by the cello.
    b. played pizzicato.   d. motivic.

437. Haydn's <u>Quartet in C Major</u>, Op. 76, No. 3 has how many movements?
    a. five   c. three
    b. four   d. two

438. Beethoven's "Pathetique" Sonata has
    a. two movements in rondo form.
    b. two movements in sonata form.
    c. three movements in sonata form.
    d. one movement in theme and variations form.

439. The form of the third movement of Beethoven's "Pathétique" Sonata can best be diagramed as
    a. ABA.   c. ABACABA.
    b. ABACA.   d. AABACCAA.

440. In Beethoven's rondo forms, the first theme usually returns in the
    a. dominant key.   c. parallel major key.
    b. tonic key.   d. subdominant key.

441. Chamber music is written for a _____ group of performers.

442. The most common type of chamber music was for the _____ _____.

443. Classical sonatas were generally written for _____.

444. In chamber music the texture is _____ and _____.

445. Many of the early string quartets were called _____.

446. Haydn's String Quartet in C Major was also called the _____ quartet.

447. _____ _____, a string quartet by Schubert, was written for piano, violin, viola, cello and string bass.

448. Sonatas with three movements usually omit the _____.

449. In the early years of the nineteenth century, _____ _____ emerged as a major composer of piano sonatas.

450. In Beethoven's piano sonata, _____ he breaks away from the Classical restrictions.

451. Christoph Willibald Gluck fought against
a. the Baroque concept of monody.
b. the idea of opera as a comic form.
c. useless and superficial musical ornaments.
d. the dramatic conventions of opera.

452. Fidelio was composed by
a. Gluck.   c. Mozart.
b. Haydn.   d. Beethoven.

453. In the Classical era, the opera orchestra was
a. very large.   c. quite small.
b. fairly large.   d. very small.

454. The male protagonist or lover in opera is frequently
portrayed by a
a. tenor.   c. bass-baritone.
b. baritone.   d. bass.

455. Which of the following operas by Mozart is a serious,
non-comic work?
a. Cosi fan tutte
b. The Marriage of Figaro
c. The Abduction from the Seraglio
d. Idomeneo

456. The term "coloratura" usually refers to which voice?
a. Soprano   c. Tenor
b. Alto   d. Bass

457. The libretto for The Marriage of Figaro was written by
a. Beaumarchais.   c. Gluck.
b. da Ponte.   d. Mozart.

458. During the Classical period, the leading masters of
opera were
a. Italian.   c. German and Austrian.
b. French.   d. English.

459. Which of the following was not composed by Haydn?
a. "Coronation" Mass   c. The Seasons
b. "Lord Nelson" Mass   d. The Creation

460. In The Marriage of Figaro, the part of Figaro is sung by a
a. countertenor.   c. baritone.
b. tenor.   d. bass.

461. The part of Susanna is sung by a(n)
    a. soprano.   c. contralto.
    b. mezzo-soprano.   d. alto.

462. The text of an opera is known as the
    a. score.   c. libretto.
    b. script.   d. synopsis.

463. In opera, the part of the older man, the authority figure,
    or villain is usually assigned to a
    a. tenor.   c. baritone.
    b. countertenor.   d. bass.

464. A cavatina is a
    a. type of recitative.   c. spoken passage.
    b. lyrical song.   d. choral movement.

465. Beethoven wrote how many operas?
    a. one   c. three
    b. two   d. four

466. The opening duet of The Marriage of Figaro involves
    a. Cherubino and Figaro.   c. Susanna and the Count.
    b. Susanna and Figaro.   d. the Count and Countess.

467. The overture to The Marriage of Figaro is in
    a. French overture form.   c. abridged sonata form.
    b. Italian overture form.   d. expanded sonata form.

468. The operatic heroine is almost always a(n)
    a. soprano.   c. contralto.
    b. mezzo-soprano.   d. alto.

469. During the Classical period,
    a. several new types of vocal music were devised.
    b. the freshest, most vital creations were found in the
        oratorio.
    c. all earlier operatic conventions were discarded as
        being "artificial."
    d. vocal music often received less attention from the
        major composers than did instrumental music.

470. Mozart died while working on his
    a. Don Giovanni.   c. Mass in C Major.
    b. Requiem Mass.   d. The Magic Flute

471. By the time _____ was writing operas, they were
    intended for _____ performance.

472. _____ is a combination of music and theater.

151

473. _____ intensifies the portrayal of the plot, characters, and emotions.

474. In an aria, the _____ is of central interest.

475. In many operas a _____ is used to present a larger mass of vocal sound.

476. A vocal ensemble in many of Mozart's operas can consist of up to _____ or more voices.

477. A _____ _____ is the first lady of the opera adored by the opera going public.

478. In opera the _____ must be heard but not over-balance the action on stage.

479. A song-play in German is called a _____.

480. _____ _____ is a comic opera in Italian.

481. Romantic artists were generally supported by
    a. universities.   c. sales of their artwork.
    b. churches.   d. city governments.

482. Typically, melody in Romantic music
    a. is subordinated to form.
    b. is very strongly emphasized.
    c. develops out of small motives.
    d. arises out of the harmony.

483. Which of the following is a typical Romantic vocal work?
    a. lied   c. symphonic poem
    b. ballade   d. nocturne

484. Generally speaking, Romantic composers were least
interested in
    a. small-scaled chamber works.
    b. serious works for band.
    c. religious music.
    d. programmatic music.

485. Werther was
    a. a German Romantic poet.
    b. a French Romantic composer
    c. the subject of a Coleridge poem.
    d. the hero of a Goethe novel.

486. Which of the following is not characteristic of
Romantic harmony?
    a. abandonment of tonality
    b. chromaticism
    c. use of remote keys
    d. dissonance

487. The nineteenth century saw the greatest technological
improvements in the
    a. strings.   c. wind instruments.
    b. organ.   d. percussion instruments.

488. The area of least experimentation throughout the Romantic
era was
    a. timbre.   c. harmony.
    b. texture.   d. rhythm.

489. The Romantic attraction to the supernatural is well demonstrated in The Rime of the Ancient Mariner by
a. Byron.
b. Dickens.
c. Coleridge.
d. Hugo.

490. The Romantic artist was chiefly interested in
a. subjective emotion.
b. objective truth.
c. overall clarity of design.
d. accuracy of detail.

491. The primary audience for Romantic music consisted of
a. the prosperous bourgeoisie.
b. peasants.
c. other artists.
d. liberals and revolutionaries.

492. The practice of continuous modulation was exploited by
a. Chopin.
b. Berlioz.
c. Schumann.
d. Wagner.

493. Don Juan was written by
a. Blake.
b. Byron.
c. Wordsworth.
d. Keats.

494. Romantic melodies are often given a new, more tragic treatment in the
a. exposition.
b. development.
c. recapitulation.
d. coda.

495. Which of the following does not apply to the archetypal Romantic hero?
a. moodiness
b. isolation
c. idealism
d. materialism

496. In the Romantic era, Classical forms became
a. unimportant.
b. more free.
c. unrecognizable.
d. more compact.

497. In general, Romantic texture is
a. similar to Medieval and Renaissance textures.
b. thinner and lighter than Classical texture.
c. chordal, with contrapuntal passages.
d. densely contrapuntal.

498. Which of the following was an important Romantic painter?
a. Delacroix
b. Goethe
c. Baudelaire
d. Fourier

499. Extramusical, programmatic associations were most frequently added to Romantic
a. chamber music.
b. études.
c. concertos.
d. symphonies.

500. Eugène Delacroix and Charles Baudelaire had a close friendship with the Romantic composer
   a. Berlioz.
   b. Chopin.
   c. Schumann.
   d. Wagner.

501. Romanticism is a way of _____ and _____ with the world.

502. Among the earliest expressions of Romanticism were found in the writings of _____.

503. With the new power and confidence of the _____ _____ a new social order had begun.

504. Romantic artists became severe _____ and _____ of society.

505. Romantic artists showed keen interest in _____ themes.

506. _____ _____ was the leading figure of French Romantic literature.

507. _____ _____ were widely used in German melodies.

508. Rhythm, like melody, in Romantic works, varies from the _____ to the _____.

509. The Romantic orchestra was larger and became a _____ instrument.

510. The first orchestra to be established in America was in the city of _____.

511. Which of the following was <u>not</u> the subtitle of a Beethoven sonata?
   a. "Sunrise"   c. "Waldstein."
   b. "Appassionata"   d. "Moonlight"

512. Liszt was <u>not</u> particularly well known for his
   a. transcriptions.   c. études.
   b. rhapsodies.   d. nocturnes.

513. The "Funeral March" Sonata was composed by
   a. Schubert.   c. Liszt.
   b. Chopin.   d. Brahms.

514. As a pianist, Liszt was primarily known for his
   a. poetic playing.   c. sight-reading ability.
   b. phenomenal memory.   d. spectacular technique.

515. Liszt's <u>Hungarian Rhapsody No. 6</u> is in the key of
   a. D^b major.   c. E^b major.
   b. D^b minor.   d. E^b minor.

516. Which of the following was <u>not</u> characteristic of Romantic piano music?
   a. Writing for the full range of the piano
   b. Composition of shorter piano works
   c. Incorporation of dance forms into piano compositions
   d. Great emphasis on a staccato style of playing

517. Which of the following composers wrote almost exclusively for the piano?
   a. Brahms   c. Chopin
   b. Schubert   d. Liszt

518. Like Chopin, Liszt settled in
   a. Paris.   c. Warsaw.
   b. Berlin.   d. Vienna.

519. Liszt's <u>Hungarian Rhapsodies</u> are based principally upon
   a. Hungarian peasant songs.
   b. Hungarian gypsy music.
   c. Medieval Hungarian ballads.
   d. dance music of the Esterházy court.

520. Once the piano had acquired a sustaining pedal, Romantic
     pianists were able to develop
     a. a smooth legato or "singing" style.
     b. brilliant dynamic effects.
     c. delicate pianissimo shadings.
     d. bright staccato effects.

521. Works that Chopin composed to illustrate and develop
     specific piano skills were his
     a. preludes.   c. études.
     b. sonatas.   d. impromptus.

522. Liszt wrote a tremendously difficult set of works called
     a. Preludes concertantes. c. Transcendental Preludes.
     b. Études concertantes.   d. Transcendental Études.

523. The nocturne was conceived by
     a. Grieg.   c. Chopin.
     b. Field.   d. Liszt.

524. The scherzo of the sonata cycle was treated as a separate
     work by
     a. Schumann.   c. Chopin.
     b. Field.   d. Liszt.

525. Chopin lived from 1810 to
     a. 1849.   c. 1871.
     b. 1856.   d. 1886.

526. A bridge between the Classical and Romantic styles is
     found in the works of
     a. Haydn.   c. Beethoven.
     b. Mozart.   d. Chopin.

527. A technique favored by Chopin in which very small
     displacements in rhythm are introduced for expressive
     purposes is called
     a. rubato.   c. legato.
     b. syncopation.   d. staccato.

528. Which of the following works for piano is not based on
     dance rhythms?
     a. mazurka   c. polonaise
     b. waltz   d. nocturne.

529. The form of Chopin's piano works is often based upon
     a. poetic form.   c. thematic repetition.
     b. sonata form.   d. programmatic connotations.

530. Particularly known for his collections of short "character" pieces was
    a. Schubert.
    b. Schumann.
    c. Chopin.
    d. Liszt.

531. In the nineteenth century composers were likely to choose _____ titles for their works.

532. Romantic composers began to write a new form of _____ literature for the piano.

533. Chopin's melodies were characterized by a _____ style.

534. _____ is a musical technique meaning to rob time in music.

535. Among Chopin's most celebrated works are his _____.

536. Among Chopin's earliest works are collections of studies called _____.

537. Particularly brilliant was Chopin's use of the _____ _____ of his native Poland.

538. Liszt's works take in a _____ part of the keyboard than his contemporaries.

539. Liszt made piano transcriptions of all nine Beethoven _____.

540. The _____ is one of the most Romantic of musical works.

541. Lieder are most commonly associated with which of the
following composers?
a. Beethoven   c. Schubert
b. Debussy   d. Brahms

542. Beethoven wrote the song cycle
a. An die ferne Geliebte.   c. Schwanengesang.
b. Frauenliebe and Leben.   d. Four Serious Songs.

543. The text of "Widmung" by Schumann concerned
a. courage in war.   c. dedication and love.
b. winter's cold.   d. fidelity and trust.

544. The Wesendonck Lieder were written by
a. Schumann.   c. Wolf.
b. Brahms.   d. Wagner.

545. Die Winterreise is based upon the poems of
a. Goethe.   c. Schiller.
b. Müller.   d. Rückert.

546. German Lieder, in comparison with the French art song,
can be best characterized as
a. introspective and profound.
b. light and elegant.
c. satiric and humorous.
d. brooding and ponderous.

547. The subject of Schubert's Die Winterreise is
a. a dying poet.
b. a girl betrayed by her lover.
c. winter hardships.
d. a rejected lover.

548. Clara Wieck was a(n)
a. Lieder singer.   c. pianist.
b. operatic singer.   d. violinist.

549. Die schöne Müllerin was composed by
a. Brahms.   c. Schumann.
b. Schubert.   d. Wieck.

550. Mahler's Das Lied von der Erde contains how many sections?
a. three   c. five
b. four   d. six

551. In his "Gute Nacht," Schubert achieved variety in all of the following ways, except through a(n)
    a. interruption by a piano cadenza.
    b. modal change from minor to major.
    c. alteration of melodic intervals.
    d. change of melodic direction.

552. Which of the following is not a song cycle?
    a. Die Winterreise
    b. Dichterliebe
    c. Lieder eines fahrenden Gesellen
    d. Widmung

553. When the music of a song is slightly altered to reflect the different texts of each stanza, the form of the song is
    a. strophic.   c. free.
    b. modified strophic.   d. theme and variations.

554. Schubert wrote Die Winterreise
    a. at the age of eighteen.
    b. in the year of his marriage.
    c. in a time of emotional stress.
    d. under the influence of Clara Wieck.

555. A particular friend of Brahms was
    a. Schubert.   c. Wolf.
    b. Schumann.   d. Mahler.

556. The concluding song of Die Winterreise is
    a. "Erlkönig."   c. "Gretchen am Spinnrade."
    b. "Gute Nacht."   d. "Der Leiermann."

557. Which of the following was not a reason for the growth of Lieder at the beginning of the Romantic period?
    a. The freedom to experiment with new forms
    b. The continued improvement of the piano
    c. The development of a new singing style
    d. The growth of Romantic lyric poetry

558. The form of Schumann's "Widmung" is
    a. ternary.   c. strophic.
    b. free.   d. modified strophic.

559. Which of the following did Schumann not write?
    a. Dichterliebe   c. Frauenliebe und Leben
    b. Schwanengesang   d. "Widmung"

560. The form of folk songs is usually
    a. strophic.   c. modified strophic.
    b. ternary.   d. free.

561. In France, the art song was called a _____.

562. Like most other songs, the German Lied combined a _____ text with _____.

563. It was _____ who first treated the Lied as a major vehicle of musical expression.

564. The new role of the _____ did much to promote the nineteenth-century emphasis on song.

565. The structure of Lieder ranged from strophic to _____ _____.

566. In German Lied there is a partnership between the _____ and the _____.

567. Schubert used much _____ writing style in his Lieder.

568. Many of Schumann's songs are explicitly _____.

569. _____ was composed by Schumann.

570. Schumann's close friend was _____.

571. Characteristically, the leading composers of abstract symphonies in the nineteenth century attempted to
    a. evoke the mood of the bygone Classical era.
    b. creates new forms for Classical ideas.
    c. express their ideas within a generally Classical framework.
    d. create wholly new, disciplined forms for the new Romantic ideas.

572. Brahms' Third Symphony is in the key of
    a. D major.   c. B minor.
    b. F major.   d. C minor.

573. The symphonies of Brahms represent a synthesis of
    a. the Classical ideal and the Romantic spirit.
    b. Baroque ornamentation and Classical symmetry.
    c. the Romantic spirit and post-Romantic technique.
    d. Romantic and Renaissance elements.

574. The nationalistic school of Russian composers did <u>not</u> include
    a. Borodin.   c. Rimsky-Korsakov.
    b. Mussorgsky.   d. Tchaikovsky.

575. The development of the program symphony is most often associated with
    a. Berlioz and Liszt.   c. Franck and Bruckner.
    b. Mahler and Strauss.   d. Beethoven and Schubert.

576. In his "Pathétique" Symphony, Tchaikovsky used the unusual meter of
    a. $\frac{5}{8}$.   c. $\frac{7}{8}$.
    b. $\frac{5}{4}$.   d. $\frac{7}{4}$.

577. Romantic composers were most innovative in their treatment of
    a. the abstract symphony and concerto.
    b. the abstract symphony and chamber music.
    c. the concerto and piano music.
    d. piano music and songs.

578. Which of the following was <u>not</u> an associate of Brahms?
    a. Anton Rubinstein   c. Joseph Joachim
    b. Clara Schumann   d. Robert Schumann

579.Tchaikovsky's "Pathétique" Symphony ends
  a. in a mood of "triumph" over fate.
  b. with a courageous march.
  c. with a low, despairing movement.
  d. in a mood of quiet resignation.

580.Which of the following works by Tchaikovsky is not a
   ballet?
  a. Swan Lake   c. Nutcracker
  b. Romeo and Juliet   d. Sleeping Beauty

581.Brahms was most profoundly inspired by
  a. Handel and Mozart.   c. Handel and Beethoven.
  b. Bach and Mozart.   d. Bach and Beethoven.

582.Mendelssohn's symphonies do not include the
  a. "Reformation."   c. "Unfinished."
  b. "Italian."   d. "Scottish."

583.Tchaikovsky's Violin Concerto in D Major was
  a. at first criticized as unplayable.
  b. at first criticized as too revolutionary.
  c. immediately recognized as a great work.
  d. the first to use "double stopping."

584.Brahms was born in
  a. Vienna.   c. Hamburg.
  b. Munich.   d. Bonn.

585.Tchaikovsky's life was roughly contemporary with that of
  a. Schumann.   c. Schubert.
  b. Brahms.   d. Mendelssohn.

586.As a composer of songs, Schubert
  a. owed little to his predecessors.
  b. was more prolific than Beethoven.
  c. was out of his element.
  d. was a transitional figure.

587.Schumann wrote how many symphonies?
  a. four   c. eight
  b. five   d. nine

588.Brahms wrote how many symphonies?
  a. three   c. five
  b. four   d. six

589.Mahler's music is sometimes considered
  a. Neobaroque.   c. post-Romantic.
  b. nationalistic.   d. avant-garde.

163

590. Which of the following late Romantic composers are known for the large scale of their symphonic works?
    a. Berlioz and Liszt
    b. Brahms and Schumann
    c. Tchaikovsky and Rachmaninoff
    d. Bruckner and Mahler

591. In his symphonic writing, _____ was very influenced by his predecessors.

592. Schubert's unfinished symphony contains _____ movements.

593. Texture in the symphony of the Romantic age became _____.

594. Romantic melodies often undergo _____ and _____ rather than Classical development.

595. Brahms best known choral work is _____ _____ _____.

596. The Nutcracker Ballet was written by _____.

597. Romeo and Juliet, like many Romantic works was inspired by _____.

598. _____ became very important in the Romantic concerto.

599. When a violinist plays two strings at once it is called _____ _____.

600. _____ had become one of the most important aspects of the nineteenth-century.

601. Program music is
  a. any music associated with nonmusical ideas.
  b. instrumental music associated with nonmusical ideas.
  c. nearly always based on a literary work.
  d. difficult to enjoy if one does not know the program.

602. Felix Mendelssohn was
  a. born to wealth and adulation.
  b. the son of an accomplished horn player.
  c. rather selfishly concerned with his own career.
  d. not a pianist, but wrote well for the piano.

603. A work of Beethoven that can properly be called
     programmatic is his
  a. Fidelio.   c. Symphony No. 6.
  b. An die ferne Geliebte.   d. Missa solemnis.

604. Which of the following is not a movement from Berlioz'
     Symphonie fantastique?
  a. "In the country"
  b. "Dream of a witches' sabbath"
  c. "March to the scaffold"
  d. "Death and transfiguration"

605. The symphonic poem
  a. is usually shorter than the program symphony.
  b. is usually longer than the tone poem.
  c. usually contains three movements, omitting the
      scherzo.
  d. contains at least one major section in sonata form.

606. The program of Danse macabre is based on a poem by
  a. Goethe.   c. Hugo.
  b. Muller.   d. Cazalis.

607. A revival of Bach's Saint Matthew Passion was organized by
  a. Mendelssohn.   c. Liszt.
  b. Berlioz.   d. Brahms.

608. The Overture to Mendelssohn's A Midsummer Night's Dream is
     in what form?
  a. scherzo   c. rondo
  b. sonata   d. free

609. The Romantic period produced relatively few
  a. symphonic poems.   c. abstract symphonies.
  b. overtures.   d. program symphonies.

610. Strauss was
    a. little interested in furthering the cause of German music.
    b. involved in a famous love affair with Harriet Smithson.
    c. a major composer of symphonic poems and operas.
    d. an accomplished horn player.

611. Mendelssohn did not compose
    a. Calm Sea and Prosperous Voyage.
    b. Songs Without Words.
    c. Fingal's Cave.
    d. Egmont.

612. A work originally to be entitled "Episode from the Life of an Artist" was
    a. the Symphonie fantastique.
    b. Les Préludes.
    c. Till Eulenspiegel.
    d. the Faust Symphony.

613. The creator of the symphonic poem was
    a. Berlioz.   c. Liszt.
    b. Mendelssohn.   d. Tchaikovsky.

614. Which of the following is a symphonic poem?
    a. Calm Sea and Prosperous Voyage.
    b. Les Préludes.
    c. A Midsummer Night's Dream.
    d. Symphonie fantastique.

615. An unusual tuning of a string instrument is called
    a. pizzicato.   c. scordatura.
    b. arco.   d. staccato.

616. In Danse macabre, Saint-Saëns includes a transformed version of
    a. "Dies irae."   c. a French folk tune.
    b. "L'Homme armé."   d. an idée fixe of Berlioz.

617. Berlioz' Harold in Italy was inspired by a poem written by
    a. Lamartine.   c. Shakespeare.
    b. Goethe.   d. Byron.

618. Which of the following were the most successful Romantic composers of program symphonies?
    a. Mendelssohn and Tchaikovsky
    b. Liszt and Berlioz
    c. Liszt and Strauss
    d. Strauss and Wagner

619. Danse macabre includes prominent solo passages for
   a. trumpet.   c. cello.
   b. horn.   d. violin.

620. The overall form of Danse macabre is
   a. rondo.   c. ternary.
   b. sonata.   d. theme and variations.

621. The nineteenth century was a time of close relationships between the _____.

622. In program music, the composers would often include _____ _____ in concert programs.

623. It was Liszt who coined the term _____ _____ to define pieces with a narrative or descriptive content.

624. One of the most important inspirations for program music was the _____.

625. Music written to accompany performed drama is called _____ _____.

626. Program symphonies could contain _____ or _____ than the usual four movements.

627. _____ _____ means fixed idea.

628. _____ _____ is the greatest of Berlioz operas.

629. The symphonic poem is essentially a program symphony in _____ movement.

630. The familiar theme of 2001 was written by Richard Strauss and is entitled _____ _____ _____.

631. Romantic elements already manifested in Mozart's opera
Don Giovanni include
   a. an emphasis on pastoral effects.
   b. a contrast of two conflicting principles.
   c. glorification of the common people.
   d. the selflessness of a persecuted rebel.

632. The operas Nabucco, Il Trovatore, and Macbeth were
composed by
   a. Leoncavallo.   c. Verdi.
   b. Puccini.   d. Rossini.

633. Jacques Offenbach wrote
   a. Orphée aux enfers.   c. Samson et Dalila.
   b. Mignon.   d. Manon.

634. In Verdi's La Traviata, the aria "Ah, fors' è lui" is
sung by
   a. Mimi.   c. Alfredo.
   b. Violetta.   d. Rudolfo.

635. Berlioz' L'Enfance du Christ is a(n)
   a. lyric opera.   c. cantata.
   b. opera.   d. oratorio.

636. An important French Romantic opera with a Spanish setting
is
   a. Carmen.   c. Les Troyens.
   b. Manon.   d. Faust.

637. Nineteenth-Century Italian opera
   a. almost completely escaped Romantic influence.
   b. gradually became both more cosmopolitan and less
       national.
   c. gradually became both more cosmopolitan and more
       national.
   d. declined from its status in the previous century.

638. Les Huguenots was a grand opera written by
   a. Offenbach.   c. Massenet.
   b. Gounod.   d. Meyerbeer.

639. A famous "mad scene" which contains some extremely
elaborate and difficult writing for solo voice, is part
of Donizetti's opera
   a. Don Pasquale.   c. Lucia di Lammermoor.
   b. Lucrezia Borgia.   d. Norma.

640. An opera for which Verdi not only composed the music but also wrote the dialogue and planned most of the scenes was
a. La Traviata.
b. Rigoletto.
c. Otello.
d. Aïda.

641. In which of the following did Wagner combine the grand opera trappings of Rienzi and the idea of redemption portrayed in Der fliegende Holländer?
a. Tannhäuser
b. Lohengrin
c. Die Meistersinger
d. Parsifal

642. An opera depicting life among struggling artists and writers in Paris is
a. La Bohème.
b. Cavalleria rusticana.
c. Rigoletto.
d. Madama Butterfly.

643. In Bizet's Carmen, the title role is sung by a(n)
a. tenor.
b. soprano.
c. mezzo-soprano.
d. alto.

644. What composer, perhaps more than any other, determined the direction in which grand opera would evolve?
a. Beethoven
b. Meyerbeer
c. Berlioz
d. Verdi

645. Puccini's operas do not include
a. La Bohème.
b. Madama Butterfly.
c. Turandot.
d. I Pagliacci.

646. Wagner's first major opera was
a. Das Liebesverbot.
b. Die Meistersinger.
c. Rienzi.
d. Tannhäuser.

647. Rossini and Verdi both wrote operas based on the story of
a. Othello.
b. Faust.
c. Caesar.
d. Falstaff.

648. Wagner's Ring of the Nibelung contains the opera
a. Rienzi.
b. Parsifal.
c. Tannhäuser.
d. Siegfried.

649. The "Ride of the Valkyries" is from the opera
a. Parsifal.
b. Das Rheingold.
c. Die Wälkure.
d. Die Götterdämmerung.

650. Perhaps the single most important grand opera in the nineteenth century was
a. Robert le Diable.
b. Les Troyens.
c. Fidelio.
d. Samson et Dalila.

651. Italian opera stressed the purely _____ aspect of the form.

652. German opera concentrated on the _____ and _____ by means of the orchestra.

653. In France, the appetite for spectacle contributed to the development of _____ _____.

654. Italian operatic recitatives are increasingly accompanied by an _____ rather than basso continuo.

655. Most German operas had scenes of village life which incorporated _____ melodies.

656. German Romantic opera had its first great flowering under the leadership of _____.

657. In German Romantic opera the role of the _____ is expanded.

658. "The Ring of the Nibelung," a cycle of four operas was written over a period of _____ years.

659. Larger choral works were generally based on traditional types, the _____ and _____

660. Many of the larger choral works were written for the _____ _____ rather than for the Church.

CHAPTER 23 NATIONALISM AND LATE ROMANTICISM

661. The term "Nationalism" was first applied to a style of
    a. painting.   c. sculpture.
    b. poetry.   d. music.

662. Which of the following is <u>not</u> a movement from Mussorgsky's <u>Pictures at an Exhibition</u>?
    a. "The Old Castle"
    b. "In the Hall of the Mountain King"
    c. "Two Polish Jews, One Rich, One Poor"
    d. "Speaking to the Dead in a Dead Language"

663. The melodies of nationalistic music were inspired by
    a. folk songs.   c. harmony.
    b. irregular meters.   d. traditional scales.

664. Which of the following was <u>not</u> a member of the Russian Five?
    a. Glinka   c. Mussorgsky
    b. Borodin   d. Rimsky-Korsakov

665. French and Italian musical styles prevailed in Europe until which century?
    a. sixteenth   c. eighteenth
    b. seventeenth   d. nineteenth

666. Edvard Grieg was a nationalist composer from
    a. Finland.   c. England.
    b. Bohemia.   d. Norway.

667. A practice common to both the late Romantics and the Impressionists was the use of
    a. Leitmotivs.
    b. chromaticism.
    c. basically contrapuntal textures.
    d. massive orchestral sound.

668. Which of the following wrote an opera that became the Czech national opera?
    a. Dvořák   c. Cui
    b. Sibelius   d. Smetana

669. In general, late Romantic music
    a. moderated the distinctive Romantic impulse.
    b. exaggerated the distinctive Romantic impulse.
    c. adopted some of the innovations of Impressionism.
    d. became almost wholly programmatic.

670. The "Symphony of a Thousand" was composed by
a. Mahler.   c. Sibelius.
b. Strauss.   d. Schoenberg.

671. Which of the following was inspired by the Kalevala myths
of his native country?
a. Smetana   c. Sibelius
b. Mussorgsky   d. MacDowell

672. Which of the following was not a characteristic of
Nationalism?
a. dance rhythms   c. new harmonic progressions
b. national instruments   d. small orchestras

673. Which of the following was a Spanish Nationalistic
composer?
a. Mussorgsky   c. Albéniz
b. Smetana   d. Elger

674. Mahler's Lieder eines fahrenden Gesellen ("Songs of the
Wayfarer") has
a. three songs.   c. six songs.
b. four songs.   d. five songs.

675. Which of the following was composed by Dvořák?
a. Má Vlast   c. Slavonic Dances
b. Russlan and Ludmilla   d. Lyric Suite

676. An interest in the speech quality of music was particularly apparent in the work of
a. Sibelius.   c. Rimsky-Korsakov.
b. Mussorgsky.   d. Glinka.

677. The Enigma Variations were composed by
a. Delius.   c. Vaughan Williams.
b. MacDowell.   d. Elgar.

678. Isaac Albéniz is perhaps best known today for the piano
pieces in a work called
a. Nights in the Gardens of Spain.
b. The Three-Cornered Hat.
c. Iberia.
d. Evening in Granada.

679. The composer of the opera Boris Godunov was
a. Mussorgsky.   c. Glinka.
b. Ravel.   d. Smetana.

680. Arnold Schoenberg's early works are best characterized as
a. Impressionist.   c. Romantic.
b. serial.   d. late Romantic.

681. National contrasts in musical style began as early as _____.

682. The nationalistic music of the nineteenth century focused upon the nation or region's _____ _____.

683. _____ _____ and their rhythms were often used by composers.

684. Glinka wrote early nationalistic _____ opera.

685. The most original of the Five was _____.

686. "Pictures at an Exhibition" was originally written for _____.

687. A Czech composer who was director of the National Conservatory in New York from 1892-95 was _____.

688. A popular work by _____ _____ is "Fantasia on Greensleeves."

689. The most important Norwegian composer was _____.

690. _____ was one of the most important aspects of style among late Romantic composers.

691. The artistic works of the Cubists and the Fauves
    a.   were inspired by the First World War.
    b.   show a strong interest in technology.
    c.   represent a repudiation of ordinary reality.
    d.   are filled with images of anxiety and torment.

692. An early twentieth-century style that stressed counter-
    point, order, and clarity of form is often referred to as
    a.   serialism.   c.   Neoclassicism.
    b.   Neoromanticism.   d.   formalism.

693. The term "Impressionism" was first applied to a style of
    a.   painting.   c.   sculpture.
    b.   poetry.   d.   music.

694. The doctrine that "form follows function" was particularly
    strong in early twentieth-century
    a.   architecture.   c.   poetry.
    b.   painting.   d.   music.

695. The group of French composers who adopted irony and humor
    as a means of ridding music of Impressionistic obscurity
    and Romantic bombast were known as
    a.   "The Five."   c.   the Neoclassicists.
    b.   "The Six."   d.   the Futurists.

696. Cubist painting originated in the works of
    a.   Matisse.   c.   Miro.
    b.   Dali.   d.   Picasso.

697. A musical style indigenous to the United States that was
    incorporated in the music of composers such as Schoenberg,
    Milhaud, and Stravinsky is
    a.   folk music.   c.   jazz.
    b.   spirituals.   d.   rock.

698. Composers who claimed that noise was the true aesthetic
    object of modern music were part of the movement known as
    a.   experimentalism.   c.   Cubism.
    b.   Futurism.   d.   objectivism.

699. Mallarmé, Rimbaud, Maeterlinck, and Verlaine were all
    a.   Impressionist composers.
    b.   Impressionist painters.
    c.   Symbolist poets.
    d.   Symbolist novelists.

700. One of the originators of modern dance was
    a. Martha Graham.   c. Luigi Russolo.
    b. Edgard Varèse.   d. Max Ernst.

701. Hindemith espoused a concept of Gebrauchsmusik, or
    a. modernism.   c. Neoromanticism.
    b. functional music.   d. experimental music.

702. Which of the following did not take place between 1914 and 1949?
    a. The Russian Revolution   b. The Spanish-American War
    b. The Chinese Revolution   c. The Spanish Civil War

703. Which of the following was not characteristic of Impressionism?
    a. avoidance of large orchestras
    b. use of parallel chords
    c. exploitation of timbre
    d. use of the whole-tone scale

704. Which of the following was an English Impressionist composer?
    a. Elgar   c. MacDowell
    b. Delius   d. Vaughan Williams

705. A tendency to avoid creating or referring to a tonal center is called
    a. pantonality.   c. serialism.
    b. atonality.   d. chromaticism.

706. Ravel's Daphnis et Chloé is
    a. an opera.   c. incidental music.
    b. a tone poem.   d. a ballet score.

707. The direct harmonic precursor of serialism was
    a. the major-minor system.
    b. the whole-tone scale.
    c. the pentatonic scale.
    d. atonality.

708. It was difficult for many early twentieth-century composers to use Classical forms, because the forms
    a. depended so heavily on major-minor tonality.
    b. were too time-worn to sustain interest.
    c. were too long for twentieth-century listeners.
    d. were too elaborate for twentieth-century listeners.

709. A short, often repeated melodic pattern is called a(n)
    a. pizzicato.   c. ostinato.
    b. rubato.   d. staccato.

710. Neoclassicism originated shortly after
    a. the turn of the century.
    b. World War I.
    c. World War II.
    d. 1960.

711. In terms of material progress, the world began moving at a fast pace at the beginning of the _____ century.

712. Straddling the nineteenth and twentieth century was the _____ movement.

713. The early years of the twentieth century saw the evolution of _____ _____.

714. Expressionism is often used to identify _____ and _____ music.

715. There was an increased interest in rhythm of the early twentieth century as pertains to _____ sounds.

716. A composer who in many respects typifies the Neoromantic style is _____.

717. The Neoclassical side of traditionalism can be seen in the work of _____.

718. Debussy wrote in a floating, unresolved _____ style.

719. There was an _____ use of dissonance in Impressionistic music.

720. Form in impressionistic music became _____.

721. The compositional elements that both Bartók and Stravinsky often stressed above all others were
   a. melody and melodic development.
   b. rhythm and percussive effects.
   c. textural richness and density.
   d. counterpoint and carefully developed form.

722. Stravinsky's works do <u>not</u> include
   a. <u>Les Noces</u>.   c. <u>King David</u>.
   b. <u>Oedipus Rex</u>.   d. <u>Symphony of Palms</u>.

723. Hindemith's treatment of melody and rhythm most often reflects his training in
   a. music from all over the world.
   b. folk music and dance.
   c. modern musical techniques.
   d. early German music.

724. Bartók was born in
   a. Hungary.   c. Russia.
   b. Bohemia.   d. Germany.

725. The beginning of Stravinsky's Neoclassical phase was marked by
   a. <u>The Firebird</u>.   c. <u>Petrouchka</u>.
   b. <u>Oedipus Rex</u>.   d. <u>Pulcinella</u>.

726. The first movement of Bartók's <u>Music for Strings, Percussion and Celesta</u> is in what form?
   a. sonata   c. free rondo
   b. fugue   d. ternary

727. Copland's ballets do <u>not</u> include
   a. <u>Woodland Sketches</u>.   c. <u>Rodeo</u>.
   b. <u>Billy the Kid</u>.   d. <u>Appalachian Spring</u>.

728. Bartók's works do <u>not</u> include
   a. <u>Concerto for the Left Hand</u>.
   b. <u>Concerto for Orchestra</u>.
   c. <u>Out of Doors Suite</u>.
   d. <u>Mikrokosmos</u>.

729. A polychord, a favorite device of Hindemith, is a
   a. chord composed of six or more tones.
   b. composite of two or more triads.
   c. chord related to two or more tonalities.
   d. composite of two or more dissonant intervals.

730. Bartók's music is
    a. seldom contrapuntal.   c. rhythmically complex.
    b. innovative in form.   d. limited in timbre.

731. Sergei Diaghilev was most closely connected with the work
    of
    a. Stravinsky.   c. Ravel.
    b. Prokofiev.   d. Shostakovich.

732. Stravinsky died in the year
    a. 1937.   c. 1963.
    b. 1945.   d. 1971.

733. Hindemith, by his own account, differed from many of his
    progressive contemporaries in his use of
    a. melody.   c. rhythm.
    b. harmony.   d. form.

734. Stravinsky's first major success was
    a. Petrouchka.   c. The Rite of Spring.
    b. The Firebird.   d. Pulcinella.

735. Bartók frequently used a melodic device known as
    a. melodic displacement.   c. octave displacement.
    b. tonal displacement.   d. harmonic displacement.

736. Hindemith resembled the Classical composers in that he
    also
    a. believed in order and symmetry.
    b. wrote many symphonies.
    c. rejected Baroque forms.
    d. had strong nationalistic tendencies.

737. Which of the following early twentieth-century composers
    was not French?
    a. Satie   c. Poulenc
    b. Britten   d. Saint-Saëns

738. The form of a Bartók work often seems to grow out of the
    a. repetition and variation of a long melody.
    b. transposition of material from one scale to another.
    c. development of very short motives.
    d. timbral variation of rhythmic themes.

739. Ives' "Fourth of July" is a
    a. serial composition.
    b. Neoclassical composition.
    c. bitonal, dissonant composition.
    d. Futurist composition.

740. Bartók's mature compositions were most influenced by the music of
   a. Mahler.
   b. Debussy.
   c. Ravel.
   d. Stravinsky.

741. In his youth, _____ was caught up in the Hungarian Nationalistic movement.

742. Bartók's melodies tend to be fairly _____.

743. Bartók used _____, a type of rhythmic counterpoint.

744. Stravinsky moved from musical _____ to _____ throughout his life.

745. Stravinsky's best known works are his _____.

746. _____ had a strong opposition to extreme harmonic innovation.

747. Innovation in the use of tonality is a primary element in the music of the American composer _____.

748. Copland's early works use _____ rhythms.

749. Copland also used _____ tunes and settings in his works.

750. Prokofiev's _____ is one of his best works written in Neoclassical style.

751. Schoenberg introduced a melodic style, notated with x's through the note stems, which tell the singer not to sustain pitches but to slide from to another; this style is called
    a. Sprechstimme.
    b. Klangfarbenmelodie.
    c. Hauptstimme.
    d. Nebenstimme.

752. Expressionism in painting arose out of
    a. Impressionism.
    b. Cubism.
    c. Fauvism.
    d. Pointillism.

753. Schoenberg's first work based entirely on a single tone row was
    a. Pierrot lunaire.
    b. Verklärte Nacht.
    c. Lyric Suite.
    d. Suite for Piano.

754. A tone row played upside down is called a(n)
    a. transposition.
    b. inversion.
    c. retrograde.
    d. retrograde inversion.

755. Berg's use of serial techniques was
    a. stricter than Schoenberg's.
    b. more Classically oriented than Schoenberg's.
    c. more lyrical than Schoenberg's.
    d. less lyrical then Webern's.

756. In the strictest use of serial techniques, immediate repetition of notes
    a. occurs sparingly.
    b. occurs frequently.
    c. occurs only in transposition.
    d. does not occur.

757. Schoenberg was very closely associated with an artistic movement called
    a. Expressionism.
    b. Cubism.
    c. Impressionism.
    d. Surrealism.

758. The twelve-tone row was
    a. completely new with Schoenberg.
    b. first developed by Schoenberg into a coherent system.
    c. formulated by Schoenberg, but developed into a coherent system by Webern.
    d. never developed into a completely coherent system.

759. Webern wrote most extensively for
  a. the voice.
  b. moderate-sized orchestra.
  c. solo instruments and small ensembles.
  d. the operatic stage.

760. Pierrot lunaire derives its text from the poems of
  a. Albert Giraud.   c. Max Beckmann.
  b. Georg Büchner.   d. Emil Nolde.

761. Two terms used by Berg and Schoenberg to designate the principal and secondary voices in a work are
  a. Sprechstimme and Klangfarbenmelodie.
  b. Hauptstimme and Nebenstimme.
  c. Sprechstimme and Hauptstimme.
  d. Nebenstimme and Sprechstimme.

762. A texture in which single notes or very short motives follow one another in quick succession in different voices, and in a higher or lower register, is called
  a. Sprechstimme.   c. a tone row.
  b. Klangfarbenmelodie.   d. pointillistic.

763. Berg's Lyric Suite contains how many movements?
  a. two   c. six
  b. four   d. eight

764. Wozzeck is an opera composed by
  a. Schoenberg.   c. Webern.
  b. Berg.   d. Büchner.

765. A technique of Schoenberg in which each note of a melody is given to a different instrument is called
  a. Sprechstimme.   c. Nebenstimme.
  b. Hauptstimme.   d. Klangfarbenmelodie.

766. Webern's Symphony, Op. 21 is scored for a
  a. small chamber orchestra.
  b. string quartet.
  c. symphony orchestra.
  d. string orchestra.

767. In the strict serial style, chords
  a. are never used.
  b. may be used only infrequently.
  c. may be used freely, if developed from the tone row.
  d. may be freely devised to support the tone row.

768. Pierrot lunaire is a good example of Schoenberg's
  a. atonal style.   c. late Romantic style.
  b. serial style.   d. chromatic style.

769. The atonality developed by Schoenberg was a(n)
   a. outgrowth of Neoclassicism.
   b. outgrowth of certain developments in late nineteenth-century harmony.
   c. reversal of the direction of late nineteenth-century harmony.
   d. outgrowth of his interest in non-Western music.

770. Including transpositions, how many forms are available for any tone row?
   a. twelve   c. forty-eight
   b. twenty-four   d. ninety-six

771. The music of _____ and _____ greatly influenced Schoenberg.

772. The subjective reality of expressionistic paintings was seldom a _____ one.

773. Atonality means _____ _____.

774. Many of Schoenberg's vocal pieces are written for _____.

775. A tone row played backwards is called _____.

776. In the serial technique there is a completely new _____ language.

777. Webern's style was much more _____ in its organization and economy of means.

778. The texture of Webern's works are at times _____.

779. Webern's use of a tone row was _____.

780. The serial technique has proven to be a _____ to modern music writing.

781. An important innovative composer and teacher of harmony
in Paris after World War II was
a. Pierre Boulez.   c. Olivier Messiaen.
b. Karlheinz Stockhausen. d. Nadia Boulanger.

782. Schoenberg's Pierrot lunaire is an early example of
modern innovations in
a. song structure.   c. accompaniment techniques.
b. vocal techniques.   d. instrumental techniques.

783. Among traditional instruments, one whose range of pitch
and timbre has particularly interested contemporary
composers is the
a. flute.   c. viola.
b. clarinet.   d. horn.

784. A composer who has worked independently of most trends in
his search for new principles of musical structure is
a. Pierre Boulez.   c. Milton Babbitt.
b. Samuel Barber.   d. Elliott Carter.

785. Pierre Boulez made us of tonal serialization in a work
called
a. Modes de valeurs et d'intensités.
b. Structures.
c. Of Wood and Brass.
d. Zeitmasse.

786. A contemporary composer who believes that things should
be allowed to "be themselves" and that noise becomes
music if properly listened to is
a. John Cage.   c. George Crumb.
b. Luciano Berio.   d. Henry Cowell.

787. Synthesized music is best described as music
a. employing electronic modification of natural sounds.
b. played on electronic instruments.
c. composed with the use of electronic apparatus.
d. created by a computer.

788. Earle Brown's chance work inspired by the mobiles of
Alexander Calder is entitled
a. Variations III.   c. Intersection No. 1.
b. 25 Pages.   d. Circles.

789. A versatile composer who began experimenting with serial techniques in his late works was
a. Stockhausen.   c. Webern.
b. Babbitt.   d. Stravinsky.

790. The notion of intervals of duration was devised by
a. Milton Babbitt.   c. Pierre Boulez.
b. Elliot Carter.   d. Earle Brown.

791. Musique concrète is distinguished by its use of
a. sounds created by synthesizer.
b. noise sounds.
c. sounds recorded on tape and electronically modified.
d. electronic and live sounds together.

792. John Cage's 4'33" was written for
a. no instrument.   c. percussion instruments.
b. flute.   d. piano.

793. The work Stravinsky called his "most advanced" was
a. Movements for Piano and Orchestra.
b. Cantata.
c. Les Noces.
d. L'Histoire du soldat.

794. Most modern innovations in vocal technique have been designed to achieve a more
a. musical effect.   c. theatrical effect.
b. dynamic effect.   d. virtuosic effect.

795. Electronic synthesizers
a. have tended to become less complex in recent years.
b. have tended to become more standardized in recent years.
c. make composition much less laborious than it formerly was.
d. began to come into vogue in the 1950s.

796. Boulez' Structures is scored for
a. piano.   c. piano and harpsichord.
b. two pianos.   d. piano and orchestra.

797. Ancient Voices of Children was composed by
a. George Crumb.   c. Earle Brown.
b. Luciano Berio.   d. Elliot Carter.

798. Stravinsky's Les Noces was particularly innovative in its use of
a. serial technique.   c. electronic synthesis.
b. musique concrète.   d. percussion instruments.

799. The new importance of dynamics, timbre, and rhythm in contemporary music has led to an increasingly important role for the
a. woodwinds.
b. brasses.
c. strings.
d. percussion instruments.

800. Which of the following composers has made frequent use of bird calls?
a. Boulez
b. Messiaen
c. Stockhausen
d. Cage

801. A harmony professor in Paris by the name of _____ was influential as a composer and teacher.

802. Within Messiaen's works _____ _____ was born.

803. Many influences can be seen in Boulez, such as _____ music.

804. Serial techniques are found only in the _____ works of Stravinsky.

805. One of the reasons composers have turned to electronic music is the limitation of _____ instruments.

806. Another innovation of electronic music is the use of the _____ .

807. In a prepared piano, John Cage would _____ the strings.

808. Glissandos, low notes, and pizzicato techniques are new to the _____ in the atonal style.

809. The type of form used in music of the later twentieth century was _____ form.

810. Another new type of form is called Aleatoric or _____ music.

811. The most important non-European influence on American music has probably been the music of
a. Africa.   c. Latin America.
b. the Orient.   d. the American Indian.

812. A jazz-related style that developed in the 1980s and reached its peak of popularity in the early twentieth century was called
a. bop.   c. boogie-woogie.
b. ragtime.   d. honky-tonk.

813. Country music developed first in the
a. Northeast.   c. South.
b. Northwest.   d. Far West.

814. A musical counterpart to black nationalism in the 1960s was
a. black folk music.   c. blues rock.
b. soul music.   d. the folk-protest song.

815. Two leading rock groups in the 1960s, representing the main divergent styles, were
a. the Beatles and the Rolling Stones
b. the Comets and the Beatles.
c. the Rolling Stones and the Jefferson Airplane.
d. The Beatles and the Who.

816. The earliest popularizer of musical comedy was
a. Irving Berlin.   c. Jerome Kern.
b. John Philip Sousa.   d. George M. Cohan.

817. The typical "big band" of the 1940s had how many players?
a. ten to twelve   c. twenty to twenty-five
b. fifteen to eighteen   d. thirty to forty

818. The "blue notes" of the blues scale are the
a. third and fifth.   c. third and seventh.
b. third and sixth.   d. fifth and seventh.

819. The gospel hymn rose to popularity in connection with a Protestant revival in the
a. 1820s.   c. 1890s.
b. 1850s.   d. 1920s.

820. Which of the following was written by Rodgers and Hammerstein?
a. South Pacific.   c. West Side Story.
b. My Fair Lady.   d. Anything Goes.

821. The most uniquely American of Anglo-American folk songs
     are
     a. patriotic songs.   c. love songs.
     b. lullabies.   d. tall tales.

822. The music for Oklahoma! was written by
     a. Rodgers.   c. Kern.
     b. Romberg.   d. Berlin.

823. The use of rhythm instruments for solo work became common
     in which of the following jazz periods?
     a. big band   c. bop
     b. New Orleans   d. cool

824. Blacks began to arrive in America about
     a. 1500.   c. 1700.
     b. 1600.   d. 1800.

825. Ragtime is usually characterized by
     a. runs and arpeggios.
     b. triple meter.
     c. strong left-hand syncopation.
     d. trumpet solos.

826. The religious counterpart of the blues was
     a. the gospel hymn.   c. the spiritual.
     b. soul music.   d. the song sermon.

827. "Lining out" was connected with the performances of
     a. bop.   c. work songs.
     b. sea chanteys.   d. hymns.

828. Early rock and roll was not characterized by
     a. simple, repetitive melodies.
     b. lightly accented four-beat rhythm.
     c. elementary tonic-dominant harmony.
     d. verse and chorus form.

829. Mahalia Jackson was best known for her singing of
     a. gospel hymns.   c. blues.
     b. folk songs.   d. country music.

830. Which of the following was not a distinctly American
     musical development?
     a. jazz   c. square dancing
     b. musical comedy   d. work songs

831. The melodies of Anglo-American folk songs are _____.

832. Some of the most important characteristics of Anglo-American folk music comes from the _____ _____.

833. The usual blues song has _____ measure phrases.

834. The harmony of a blues song is based on the _____, _____, and _____ chords of a scale.

835. One of the greatest blues singers of the early twentieth century was _____ _____.

836. Minstrel shows and vaudeville were outgrowths of _____ _____ _____.

837. Jazz rhythms are strongly influenced by the rhythms of _____ _____.

838. The first important center for the new jazz styles was in _____ _____.

839. One of the jazz giants from the early decades through the 1960s was _____ _____.

840. Early rock and roll began in America in the middle _____.

CHAPTER 29   ASPECTS OF MUSIC
IN SOME NON-WESTERN CULTURES

841. Early Chinese musicians held it to be of the greatest
importance that their instruments be tuned
a. according to the laws of Confucius.
b. on the basis of the one true foundation tone.
c. to a system of equal temperament.
d. differently for ya-yueh and su-yueh.

842. Melodies in Bantu music are influenced most basically by
a. the rhythmic vitality of African music as a whole.
b. the European folk-song tradition.
c. the speech tones of the words being sung.
d. the purpose for which the song is intended.

843. The drone note in Indian music provides a basis for
a. melody.   c. textural contrast.
b. rhythm.   d. harmony.

844. The music of Central Africa is characterized by
a. rhythmic polyphony.
b. purely monophonic texture.
c. melodies covering an extremely wide pitch range.
d. a complex set of precise rhythmic formulae.

845. Melodies that undulate back and forth and a declamatory
singing style are characteristic of
a. Plains Indian music.   c. Eskimo music.
b. Pueblo Indian music.   d. Northwest Coast music.

846. The "elegant" music of Japan is based on the Chinese
ya-yueh and is known as
a. bunraku.   c. su-yueh.
b. gagaku.   d. kabuki.

847. Which of the following three notes would be likely to
form the drone chord used in an Indian raga?
a. 1-3-5   c. 1-5-8
b. 1-3-8   d. 1-6-8

848. Northwest Coast music differs from all other American
Indian music in that it
a. is solely instrumental.
b. is based on the pentatonic scale.
c. is based on the major scale.
d. includes rudimentary part singing.

849. Which of the following does <u>not</u> represent a class of Chinese instruments?
a. bone   c. metal
b. bamboo   d. gourd

850. A musical form such as AABCABC is known as
a. free.   c. free rondo.
b. incomplete repetition.   d. compound ternary.

851. Which of the following had the most influence on the musical tradition of Japan?
a. Korea   c. India
b. Manchuria   d. China

852. The ceremonial Sun Dance was an important part of tribal life among the
a. Plains Indians.   c. Eskimos.
b. Pueblo Indians.   d. Northwest Coast Indians.

853. Which of the following is <u>not</u> characteristic of the type of Chinese music known as ya-yueh?
a. refined style   c. chordal harmony
b. monosyllabic   d. not strongly rhythmic

854. The voice quality characteristic of Plains Indian singers might best be described as
a. low and growing.   c. high and nasal.
b. open and relaxed.   d. tense and pulsating.

855. Which of the following is <u>not</u> a musical instrument?
a. sitar   c. biwa
b. tala   d. samisen

856. Pueblo songs are more complex than those of the Plains and are often based on a
a. five-note scale.   c. nine-note scale.
b. seven-note scale.   d. twelve-note scale.

857. Which of the following theatrical forms involves the use of puppets?
a. bunraku   c. kabuki
b. noh   d. Peking opera

858. A distinctive result of the tonal nature of Bantu language is that
a. forms based on poetry are rarely used.
b. forms based on poetry are used almost exclusively.
c. harmony, as such, is virtually ignored.
d. instruments can be used to convey verbal meanings.

859. An important musical import into Japanese tradition was
    a. Shinto chant.   c. Ainu folk music.
    b. Buddhist chant.   d. "breath rhythm."

860. In some types of gagaku, which one of the following
    families of instruments is never used?
    a. strings   c. reeds and flutes
    b. mouth organ   d. gongs

861. Music has a variety of functions in many societies of
    the world, one is the _____.

862. In African tribal societies music is an essential part
    of _____ _____.

863. Many African Bantu rulers have had official _____.

864. Much of Bantu music is built on _____ _____ phrases.

865. When several different rhythms are played at the same
    time it is called _____ _____.

866. In the traditional songs of the Plains, melodies cover
    a _____ range.

867. The text for the first half of the Plains songs is made
    up of _____ syllables.

868. Some Northwest Coast songs were _____ by individuals.

869. Indian music is based on melodies called _____.

870. At least three hundred varieties of Chinese _____
    are known.